The Cambridge Introduction to
Margaret Atwood

Margaret Atwood offers an immensely influential voice in
contemporary literature. Her novels have been translated into over
twenty-two languages and are widely studied, taught and enjoyed.
Her style is defined by her comic wit and willingness to experiment.
Her work has ranged across several genres, from poetry to literary
and cultural criticism, novels, short stories and art. This Introduction
summarizes Atwood's canon, from her earliest poetry and her first
novel, *The Edible Woman*, through *The Handmaid's Tale* to *The Year
of the Flood*. Covering the full range of her work, it guides students
through multiple readings of her oeuvre. It features chapters on her life
and career, her literary, Canadian and feminist contexts, and how her
work has been received and debated over the course of her career.
With a guide to further reading and a clear, well-organized structure,
this book presents an engaging overview for students and readers.

Heidi Slettedahl Macpherson is Dean of the Faculty of Humanities
and Professor of English at De Montfort University, Leicester.

The Cambridge Introduction to
Margaret Atwood

HEIDI SLETTEDAHL MACPHERSON

CAMBRIDGE
UNIVERSITY PRESS

CAMBRIDGE UNIVERSITY PRESS
Cambridge, New York, Melbourne, Madrid, Cape Town, Singapore,
São Paulo, Delhi, Dubai, Tokyo, Mexico City

Cambridge University Press
The Edinburgh Building, Cambridge CB2 8RU, UK

Published in the United States of America by Cambridge University Press, New York

www.cambridge.org
Information on this title: www.cambridge.org/9780521694636

First published 2010

Printed in the United Kingdom at the University Press, Cambridge

A catalogue record for this publication is available from the British Library

Library of Congress Cataloguing in Publication data
Macpherson, Heidi Slettedahl.
    The Cambridge introduction to Margaret Atwood / Heidi Slettedahl Macpherson.
        p.   cm. – (Cambridge introductions to literature)
    Includes bibliographical references and index.
    ISBN 978-0-521-87298-0 – ISBN 978-0-521-69463-6 (pbk.)
    1. Atwood, Margaret, 1939 – Criticism and interpretation.   I. Title.   II. Series.
    PR9199.3.A8Z743 2010
    818′.5409–dc22
    2010026361

ISBN 978-0-521-87298-0 Hardback
ISBN 978-0-521-69463-6 Paperback

For Allan

Contents

Preface

Margaret Atwood has been writing poetry, fiction and criticism for almost fifty years. Her influence on Canadian literature is phenomenal, and her influence on contemporary literature as a whole is immense. Her readings fill theatres and her books win a range of literary and social prizes. She has gone from being 'world famous in Canada' (to repeat Mordecai Richler's famous joke) to being world famous, full stop.

Atwood used to find that the media tried to reinvent her in ways that she didn't recognize, and perhaps some of that reinvention continues. However, Atwood notes:

> Once you hit the granny age, people think that you may be okay and that you're handing out cookies to younger writers and waving your benevolent fairy godmother wand over the proceedings, but you're no longer the sort of threat that you were because people kind of know what you are by now. They're not expecting some awful threatening surprise to appear.

Yet Atwood continues to have the power to surprise – from embracing new genres, to developing expertise in the extra-textual side of contemporary publishing, to returning to the poetry that first made her famous. Each Atwood text is a treat, whether it spans only a few lines, or offers up an intricate puzzle in the form of a multilayered novel.

Spanning different genres, as well as crossing over them, Atwood's work appeals to academics and non-academics alike, and this introduction will give you the opportunity to explore not only her own life and work but also the contexts for it and reception of it. It references the work of a number of key Atwood scholars, of which there are many, drawn from across North America, Britain and Europe. Atwood was once told by her high school English teacher, 'This must be a very good poem dear because I can't understand it at all.' The explosion of criticism on Atwood – and this introduction – should help you to find your way through her tricky, intelligent and often comic work.

Some of this research has been made possible through the generous assistance of the Canadian Government's Faculty Research Program. I also want to thank Professor Philip Davies for giving me the opportunity to present the 2009 Eccles Lecture on Atwood at the Annual British Association for Canadian Studies Conference held in Oxford. My thanks go to Margaret Atwood for permission to quote from the interview undertaken in Toronto in August 2007 and to Rachael Walters for so faithfully transcribing the interview.

Final thanks go to my colleagues at De Montfort University, and to my family, Judy Clayton, Amy Northrop, Bob Slettedahl, Jill Winter and Allan Macpherson, for love and support.

Quotations from the poem 'You Fit Into Me' reproduced with permission of Curtis Brown Group Ltd, London on behalf of Margaret Atwood; ©Margaret Atwood 1987.

Abbreviations and note on references

Quotations will be cited in parentheses in the text by page number for Atwood's work, and parenthetically with author's name for secondary criticism. Full bibliographical information for secondary criticism cited can be found on pp. 124–32.

AG	*Alias Grace*
BA	*The Blind Assassin*
BE	*Bluebeard's Egg and Other Stories*
BH	*Bodily Harm*
CE	*Cat's Eye*
CP	*Curious Pursuits: Occasional Writing 1970–2005*
DG	*Dancing Girls and Other Stories*
EF	*Eating Fire: Selected Poetry 1965–1995*
EW	*The Edible Woman*
HT	*The Handmaid's Tale*
LM	*Life Before Man*
LO	*Lady Oracle*
MD	*Moral Disorder*
ND	*Negotiating with the Dead: A Writer on Writing*
OC	*Oryx and Crake*
PB	*Payback: Debt as Metaphor and the Shadow Side of Wealth*
RB	*The Robber Bride*
Surf	*Surfacing*
Surv	*Survival: A Thematic Guide to Canadian Literature*
SW	*Second Words: Selected Critical Prose*
T	*The Tent*
WT	*Wilderness Tips*
YF	*The Year of the Flood*

Chapter 1

Life

'If you write a book on me', Margaret Atwood claims, 'you have to have a chapter on hair'. In an interview with me in Toronto in the summer of 2007, Atwood claimed, 'I have the hair criticism. I get criticism of the book, criticism of the ascribed personality and then criticism of the hair. That's why you have to have a chapter on hair.'[1] Early photographs of Atwood do indeed focus on her remarkably curly hair – and underscore the unsurprising truth that female authors battle against a link between their appearance and their critical reception (indeed, several of the critical books on Atwood use her photograph as the front cover). If Atwood's reputation now firmly rests on her output and not her appearance, nevertheless the effects of this early focus on her looks are apparent in her critical and creative output, and show in one small way how biography necessarily has an impact upon a writer's life and her work.

Atwood's famous humour is apparent in this little vignette, as well as a number of important themes in relation to Atwood herself and her place in Canadian and world literature. A literary author's relationship to her texts (and her readers) is a matter of some critical debate, from claims that the author is the font of all knowledge to claims that readers determine meanings and from everything in between, yet fascination with details of an author's life do not seem to abate. Atwood has been the subject of two sustained biographies, both of which were published in 1998, and neither of which were authorized. Nathalie Cooke's biography, entitled simply, *Margaret Atwood: A Biography*, explores her life in detail, outlining, for example, where Atwood lived as a child and what she read, whereas Rosemary Sullivan's book, *The Red Shoes: Margaret Atwood Starting Out*, is, in her own words, a 'not-biography', focusing instead on Atwood's 'creative life' (Sullivan 2).

Margaret Eleanor Atwood was born in Ottawa, Canada, on 18 November 1939 and had an unusual early childhood, spending summers in the Canadian 'bush' because her father Carl, an entomologist, brought the family with him on his scientific explorations. She was the second of three children, and along with her older brother Harold, learned from an early age to live an alternative lifestyle, with several months of every year spent learning by doing and out of contact with most other people. Away from formal schooling for much of the time, she learned through literature, reading far above her age level, and this eclectic reading has certainly had an influence on her work, from fairy tales (in their original and harsher versions), to myth and legends from a variety of cultures. She was, as a child, also fond of comic books and pocketbook mysteries (Cooke 1998, 25). As Atwood recalls, '[N]o one ever told me I couldn't read a book. My mother liked quietness in children, and a child who is reading is very quiet' (*ND* 7). However, she also noted that '[s]tories were for twilight, and when it was raining; the rest of the time, life was brisk and practical' and included lessons on 'avoiding lethal stupidity' (*ND* 8). Atwood was a child during the Second World War, though much of it was spent in the bush; it was not until Atwood was five that she began to live primarily in cities.

Her younger sister Ruth was born in 1951, the same year that Atwood began to attend school regularly. Atwood once joked that she didn't write anything in the dark period between eight and sixteen, a flippant comment that was recycled by another interviewer who asked her why this was so (Ingersoll 66), but by sixteen, she was clear she wanted to be a writer. At the time, there was little sense of a body of work called Canadian literature, making her decision to embrace the writing life not only unusual, but improbable (doubly improbable given that she was female, too). By 1957 Atwood was at Victoria College, University of Toronto, where she obtained her Bachelor's degree, followed by a Master's degree from Radcliffe College in the USA. She began doctoral work at Harvard in 1961 but never completed her studies; her planned Ph.D. was on 'Nature and Power in the English Metaphysical Romance of the 19th and 20th Century'. She has held a number of diverse jobs – market research, waitressing, teaching – but her passion has always been creative, whether writing, illustrating comic books or painting.

In 1967 Atwood married James Polk, though by 1973 they were divorced and she began living with the writer Graeme Gibson, with whom she had worked at the House of Anansi Press, a publishing company set up specifically to publish Canadian writers. In 1976 their daughter Eleanor Jess Gibson was born. Atwood has travelled widely, living for times in the USA, France, England, Scotland, Germany and Australia. One measure of her critical and commercial appeal is that she has won a diverse range of honours, from *Ms. Magazine*'s Woman of the Year to the Norwegian Order of Literary Merit. Atwood has also won a number of prestigious literary prizes, including, amongst others, The Booker Prize, The Giller Prize and The Governor General's Award, and holds honorary doctorates from several universities including, fittingly, Harvard, as well as Cambridge, Toronto, and the Université de la Sorbonne Nouvelle, Paris. She became a Fellow of the Royal Society of Canada in 1987. With this impressive list of achievements, it is clear that Atwood is a key figure in creating – as well as disseminating – Canadian culture.

Atwood has written everything from children's books to literary and cultural criticism. Her work has been translated into over twenty-two languages and forms the basis of course syllabi from A Level to postgraduate work, and an entire academic society – The Margaret Atwood Society, with whom she has an uneasy relationship – is devoted to the study of her creative outputs. A recent Annotated Bibliography on Atwood (compiled by the Society) listed 133 scholarly works published on the author in one year alone,[2] and there are currently over 35 specialized, academic monographs or edited collections that take her as their principal or sole focus (not including books focused primarily on the teaching of Atwood's individual texts or those which explore her work in a comparative context). The annual Modern Language Association (MLA) convention reserves space for two sessions on Atwood scholarship each year. But she is more than just an author, too. Atwood invented the LongPen in 2006, a device that allows her to sign autographs remotely, fully fitting in with her green credentials and her preference to reduce her carbon footprint. Though some have worried that this might signal the demise of the book tour, these fears, so far, have been unfounded, and video-conferencing allows autograph-seekers to see and converse with the writer even when she is signing remotely.

Another measure of Margaret Atwood's influence and success resides in the Atwood Archives in the Thomas Fisher Rare Book Library at the University of Toronto that number some 369 boxes, while a description of the contents runs to 220 pages. The materials included range from juvenilia and unpublished manuscripts to early rejection letters and discussions of filmic projects based on her work. Though a number of critics have traced autobiographical resonances in her work (particularly in her 1988 novel *Cat's Eye*), Atwood herself generally insists on the distance between herself and her creations. In fact, as early as 1978 she noted how the media created images of Atwood-as-writer that may or may not have anything to do with the 'real' Margaret Atwood (citing 'Margaret the Medusa', 'Margaret the Magician' and 'Margaret the Man-eater' stereotypes in her article 'The Curse of Eve – Or, What I Learned in School'). Atwood distances herself from these creations and carefully manages her public persona, but her celebrity is a facet of life that she must continually negotiate.

If celebrity is intimately linked to biography (and autobiography), then it is no wonder that readers wish to hear Atwood's 'real' voice and are willing to purchase a collection of her writing on reading; for example, in 2005 she published a collection of 'occasional writing' entitled *Curious Pursuits*, a text that combines interviews, newspaper columns, reviews, and miscellaneous musings on everything from the act of writing to responses to world politics. Such a collection speaks to the range of writing that Atwood undertakes, as well as the scope of her reach into both academic and popular fora. As Ray Robertson notes, "Any author whose work … can be found in both airport newspaper shops *and* on graduate school syllabi all over the world must be doing something right" (quoted in Pache in Nischik 120, ellipses in original).

In purchasing or perusing such a text, the reader knows that Atwood has read the books she is commenting on within it. In this way, perhaps they feel they know her a bit more, too. Atwood claims that she is an 'addicted' reader, but also admits that she only reviews books she likes:

> As soon as I'm doing a book review … I'm reading with the little stickies that you place on to reference a page, so that you can find it again when you're doing your review. What I like to do before I say I'm going to do a review is to read the book to see whether I enjoy it enough to want to read it again, and possibly again. If the answer is no then … I can't do this. It may be a good book but I have, personally, nothing to say about it.

Thus, by reading what Atwood *does* like, it is as if the reader can ascertain what she *is* like, though in true Atwoodian form, the author resists any reading of herself at all. Indeed, during interviews, Atwood seeks to wrest control of the narrative, often in a charming, self-deprecating way. In seeking to expand on readings of her work during the interview I undertook with her, I acknowledged my own role as a reader of her work, an acknowledgement that she sought to take further. Calling me an 'instigated reader', Atwood suggested:

> Well a reader-reader is just reading and they want all the things that one does when one reads a book, including the incentive for reading the next page. You, poor creature, are shackled to the Margaret Atwood desk; you've got to turn the next page whether you want to or not.

In turning the focus on the interviewer, Atwood retained control of the dynamic; in setting the desk as a proxy for herself, she retained distance. The desk imagery is important for more than one reason, particularly as her original homepage at O. W. Toad (www.owtoad.com) featured the 'desk of Margaret Atwood', an icon that allowed for navigation – to a certain extent. In a clever reading of Atwood's website, Lorraine York notes that the site offers a sense of intimacy but manages to control access at the same time: 'As with her Web site desk graphic, Atwood's persona takes control of her desk, agreeing to open some personal spaces in a controlled atmosphere while resolutely declaring her right to keep other drawers closed' (York 114). The fact that Atwood's website was called the 'Margaret Atwood Reference Site' rather than her homepage also indicates a certain distance here, and even the biographical detail section is incomplete, with Atwood's awards, jobs and places of residence taking precedence over more intimate details. Her new website is similarly silent on personal details. In an article in Coral Ann Howell's *The Cambridge Companion to Margaret Atwood*, York suggests that Atwood has 'intervened as an active, canny agent to shape the discourses surrounding her celebrity' (Howells 2006, 28). Indeed, one desk drawer reveals comics of Atwood (with wild hair) as if in an interview situation. Discussing *Negotiating with the Dead*, Atwood's character makes fun of her interviewer, who thinks she has written a how-to book for writers:

> And this is how you write all your books?
> Absolutely! Follow these simple instructions and you too can be on talk shows! As a guest, that is.[3]

The idea of Atwood-as-guest both feeds into an awareness of celebrity and makes fun of the suggestion that such celebrity is easy to attain. Atwood's awareness of celebrity – and her refusal of it – is revealed in many of the interviews that she has undertaken, including the one with me:

> Well, let's be very frank about celebrity. I'm not a football star. I'm not a film star. I'm not a TV star. I haven't murdered anyone. I'm not a top model. I am a writer of literary fiction. And the level of fame and celebrity that you get doing that is quite manageable. You'll notice I have no bodyguards around me. No screaming fans are clambering over my shoelaces. So it's not the same kind of thing as it would be if you were Jackie Kennedy, Elizabeth Taylor, Mick Jagger, that person who plays football … David Beckham, a Spice Girl. Any of those kinds of things are at a very much higher level of that phenomenon than a person who writes books ever will be.

Atwood's list of 'real' celebrities is instructive. The fact that she includes murderers in her hierarchy of fame (and has written about the celebrity attached to crime in *Alias Grace*) shows that her sense of celebrity is not one that is confined to those whose *artistic* exploits are exploited by the media. However, the preponderance of such people in her list – football stars (and their wives), pop stars, and television and film stars – reveals the commonplace assumption that the majority of people whose lives are potentially turned upside down by fame are ones whose fame rests at least in part on their visual appeal. Atwood has also struggled with the focus on her looks, and has commented in several essays about the difficulties of being a woman writer, noting back in 1980 that '[a] man's work is reviewed for its style and ideas, but all too often a woman's is reviewed for the supposed personality of the author as based on the jacket photograph' (*SW* 331). Although it would be comforting to think that this has changed dramatically in the nearly thirty years since she wrote these words, the subject of visual impact is still very much on her mind, as noted in the flippant comments about her hair which began this introduction (and our interview).

Such replies suggest that despite her disavowal, Atwood recognizes her celebrity status. At the same time, though, she continues to insist on the distance between herself and other celebrities:

> People who read books identify with the book, not so much with you. They only identify with you if someone else writes a book in which you figure as a character like Virginia Woolf and *The Hours*; then you get to be a character in a work of fiction … So, when you're dead and you get to be a character in somebody else's book, then you can have that kind of identification with yourself, but other than that you're just the medium. People don't go to a seance to talk to the medium; they go to talk to Aunt Bessie!

Atwood's sense of herself as the medium and not the message is at odds with the still pervasive desire for autobiographical resonances that some readers attach to the author, despite the fact that many literary critics have moved away from autobiography as a legitimizing force.[4] As if to underline her resistance, a documentary which sought to uncover more about Atwood, Michael Rubbo's *Once in August* (National Film Board of Canada, 1984), shows her and her family playfully subverting that project: Atwood donned a paper bag and the amassed people asked, 'Who is this woman?'

Such self-conscious recognition of her role(s) – and the critic's desire for her exposure – is also played out in Atwood's critical and creative work. In her collection *Negotiating with the Dead* (2002), which came out of the Empson Lectures she gave at Cambridge in 2000, Atwood fleetingly refers to her own life, but more often, deflects attention away from herself and onto other writers, or to a mythical Writer who is somehow different from the person who writes. Atwood suggests, 'The author is the name on the book. I'm the other one' (*ND* 37), and the collection works hard to ensure that this kind of doubling is highlighted (with, amongst other things, its references to Jekyll and Hyde, as well as its focus on twins and doppelgängers). Atwood explores her own early biography more to dispel notions of the special writer than to reaffirm them, and she even claims:

> If I had suspected anything about the role I would be expected to fulfill, not just as a writer, but as a *female* writer – how irrevocably doomed! – I

would have flung my leaky blue blob-making ballpoint pen across the room … I would never have done any interviews, nor allowed my photo to appear on book jackets; but I was too young then to know about such ruses, and by now it is far too late.   (*ND* 15, italics in original)

Negotiating with the Dead is subtitled 'A Writer on Writing', and the very use of the indefinite article is suggestive of Atwood's simultaneous implied exposure and critical distancing. The *A* does not fix the writer's identity, but allows a non-specific reading, whilst at the same time, her name across the top of the book – in much larger letters than the title – dispels the non-specificity implied.

In another example, her interview on *The South Bank Show* (1993), which dramatizes aspects of *The Robber Bride*, shows Atwood offering tips about which muffins are the most edible as often as it speaks about her writing. Furthermore, revelations about her private life are strictly rationed, and focus on flippant remarks about previous jobs ('I've been a waitress and a critic, and believe me, it's harder being a waitress'). Emotional outpourings of her biographical secrets do not feature.

This distancing from the autobiographical aspects of writing (apart from the carefully apportioned aspects mentioned above) was somewhat overturned in 2006, when Atwood published *Moral Disorder*, a collection of linked short stories that, on the face of it at least, draws on autobiographical resonances to a larger extent than previously. Thirty years before, in an interview with Linda Sandler, Atwood noted that 'if you write a "serious" book, everybody wants it to be autobiographical' (Sandler in Ingersoll 26), and offered up the quip that Shakespeare was lucky because, since no one knew anything about him, all they had to deal with was his output. Thus, the creative decision to incorporate autobiography within a series of short stories is one that I probed in interview. Atwood suggested that she did not always refuse the autobiographical tag, only those places where it did not apply:

how much is real, how much is not real; the fact is that, sure, you always use stuff that has gone through your head, so in that sense everything's autobiographical. On the other hand, you always alter everything that goes through your head; in that sense, nothing is autobiographical because it's all been made into something else, and we do live in an age in which when you write something called an autobiography people are bound to think you're lying, and if you write something called fiction they're bound to think you're secretly telling the truth, but they're not sure just in what area you're telling the truth. But I, essentially, feel that I don't care which daffodils Wordsworth saw; I'm sure he saw some daffodils. I don't need to know exactly which ones. It's not of interest to

> me, although it might be of interest to a daffodil fancier or somebody who's really wanting to get so thoroughly into the life of William Wordsworth. So I could go through and annotate the whole thing: this is real; this is not real; this happened but not in this order; yes, we had all of these animals, but we had more animals than these, just didn't put them all in; I didn't put in all the vegetables. Any fiction is edited; you can't put everything in, and any fiction is rearranged. As people have often said, you can tell the same story about the same people from a different point of view and it would be quite different.

Thus, even in her reply, Atwood is selective, her 'this is real' is not specified; instead, Atwood suggests that life material is just that: material, to be reworked in fictional ways, and ways that she does not need to reveal. Thus, even in her most explicitly autobiographical mode, Atwood retains control. She does this in part by refusing to engage with or worry about what her readers think.

> I can't control what they think, so why would I concern myself with it? … You as a critic can suggest to them what they might think or you can suggest different ways of looking at things, and I as a novelist can do that with my characters, but you cannot tell them; you cannot reach into their little minds and twist a few knobs and have it come out the way you want.

Moreover, the delay between the point where the writing is finished and when it is published suggests to Atwood that what the readers are reading is different from what she is currently working on. She also lends yet another layer of distance by noting that she does not read current reviews, only older ones (and then, not always), to avoid getting involved in discussions with others over what other reviewers think: 'So it's nice to have wonderful reviews, it's interesting to have nasty, personal attacks, they're always peculiar and weird and you don't know where they come from, but there's nothing you can do about it; you can't control it.'

If Atwood herself suggests that celebrity is something apart from herself, her creative work engages with celebrity at several levels, from the early comic novel *Lady Oracle* (1976), which focused on Joan Foster as a reluctant celebrity poet who feels compelled to fake her own death, to the Booker Prize-winning novel *The Blind Assassin* (2000), where celebrity is wrongly attributed to Laura Chase rather than to her sister Iris, the real author of the celebrated text of the same name. In this case, Iris takes perverse pleasure in explicitly manufacturing her dead sister's celebrity and hiding behind it. In these novels, as in *Cat's Eye*, which focuses on the retrospective exhibit of the artist Elaine Risley's work, celebrity is linked figuratively to death; Elaine notes that she has 'a public face, a face worth defacing' (*CE* 20), but she also worries that a retrospective exhibition suggests death, or something like it. York notes the frequency with which Atwood links celebrity and death, and this is something that also came out of the interview I undertook. When I noted to Atwood that I thought most students would think of her primarily as a novelist (and thus sadly missing out her critical work as well as her poetry), Atwood's response was wry: 'I would think most students think of me, primarily, as a dead person ... all the people I read about in high school were dead. Why would they be different? It's rather shocking to discover some of them are still alive'.

Although it is doubtful that students are indeed shocked by Atwood's continued presence, Atwood herself appears to be surprised by the recycling of interviews conducted years before, noting that this phenomenon is

> Very peculiar because you thought at the time they were one offs and everything at the time was a one off then. When you did an interview that was the end of it, but now they are pod casting, web streaming, downloading ... you do have a virtual presence that's circulating endlessly whether you like it or not, and there's not just one alter ego out there, there's a whole pack of them.

Atwood's alter egos may follow her around, resurfacing even when the original did not air (as in the archived Hana Gartner interview, posted under the title 'Atwood Brandishes her Caustic Tongue' that was never shown, but is now streamable from the CBC website, and linked to Atwood's own),[5] but even this is not enough to convince Atwood of her own celebrity, as the following exchange makes clear:

> **Macpherson**: But I wonder if you're not underestimating your own, to use the word again, celebrity, and your own influence –
> **Atwood**: Everything's relative; with six billion people in the world, of those six billion people, how many do you think have heard of me?
> **Macpherson**: I don't know. I guess that puts it into perspective.
> **Atwood**: Millions, but not in the six billions; in fact, there's probably no person on the face of the planet who has been heard of by all six billion.
> **Macpherson**: But your readings are very popular; people flock to them.
> **Atwood**: Oh sure, as *readings*. As football games they would be considered horrible failures because only 500 people were there.
> **Macpherson**: But if that's as big as the theatre is ...
> **Atwood**: Even if there were 3,000 people you couldn't fill it; I could not fill a 3,000 people stadium, sorry.
> **Macpherson**: Don't be sorry, but I wonder again if you're not underestimating –
> **Atwood**: No, I know pretty much how things are. I could do 1,500.

> **Macpherson**: We should negotiate then. Do you think you could do 2,200?
>
> **Atwood**: I've done 2,000, but it depends where and when, and you don't want them actually to be really that big, because it's a much more intimate thing; you're not playing a game watched by millions. You're participating in an experience shared by hundreds at a time, that's how it is.

Atwood's humour is clearly much in evidence here, and there is a certain sense as York notes that Atwood herself is participating in her own celebrity even as she refuses it; she allowed herself to be negotiated 'up' to an audience figure of 2,000, though she also suggests in the interview that she is very 'Canadian' in wanting to deny her place in the hierarchy of cultural exports.

Lady Oracle's Joan Foster notes, 'It's no good thinking you're invisible if you aren't' (*LO* 12), and this reminder may well be as appropriate for Atwood as it is for her creations. The very visibility of her protagonists and their complicated relationships to fame suggest that this powerful metaphor is one that will continue to resonate for Atwood, and her readers. It is clear that links between Atwood, celebrity and auto/biography are contestable, culturally informed and likely to be denied by the author herself. If Atwood is the self-confessed 'other one', the doppelgänger of the author, she is nevertheless a recurrent subject of critical debate and conjecture, her writing offering up a narrative of Atwood as writer, cultural export and cultural commentator. In what follows I will explore Atwood's writing – both creative and critical – as well as the contexts and reception of her work.

Contexts

The most important contexts for situating the work of Margaret Atwood include her position as a Canadian writer, particularly given that she began writing at a time when a tradition of Canadian literature was not visible; her own criticism, which emerged partly out of this absence of a critical heritage; and her relationship with feminism. This chapter, in focusing on the historical, literary and cultural forces against which Atwood's work must be placed, thus begins by situating Atwood within the Canadian canon.

Consider the historical situation of Canada: it came into being as a political entity in 1867 as British North America, and only achieved absolute independence from the UK in 1982 by way of the Canada Act. Atwood had already been publishing her work for twenty years by this point. It has the USA as its southern, powerful and loud neighbour, and most Canadians live within 100 miles of the border (Corse 158), making it difficult to establish any clear *natural* distinctions between the two countries. Yet, in an era of increasing internationalization, increasing awareness of the 'otherness' of identity, Canada – at least in some literary quarters – holds fast to a sense of a Canadian identity which is separate from and clearly distinguishable from 'America'. It has two official languages, English and French, as well as multiculturalism enshrined in law, all of which militate against a singular literary canon. Moreover, in Atwood's youth, Canadians were not taught about a Canadian canon and even when she studied literature at university, Canadian literature was not on the syllabus, a fact she records in own critical work, *Survival*, as well as in numerous interviews. However, a recognizable entity called 'CanLit' has been developing ever since, and Atwood is clearly central to it, both as a creative writer and as a critic.

English-Canadian literature and the development of the canon

In his book *Worrying the Nation*, Jonathan Kertzer reiterates the truism that 'English-Canadian literary history has been distinguished by its modest but persistent nationalism, by its mistrust of foreign influences, and above all by its casual appeal to historical conditions (roughing it in the bush, the garrison) and cultural forces (colonialism, regionalism, puritanism) as guarantees of coherence and value' (3). While Kertzer rightfully takes issues with each of these suppositions, their enduring status highlights the fact that Canadian writers themselves either attempt – or are seen to attempt – the creation of a distinctively national literature.

Lorna Irvine argues that Canadian women writers are in a fortunate position, since 'they are participating in a developing literary tradition, rather than reacting to an already-established one' and thus they are able to aid in the 'creation of their country's fictional landscape' (Irvine in Davidson and Broner 242). Alongside other key English-Canadian women writers such as Alice Munro, Carol Shields, Margaret Laurence, Marian Engel and Joan Barfoot, Atwood has done just that. David Staines has gone so far as to claim: 'As Atwood discovered her voice as a Canadian writer of poetry, fiction, and literary criticism, she helped the country discover its own life as a literary landscape' (Staines in Howells 19). Whilst this may be an overstatement, according Atwood more power than she would wish to accept, Staines' linkage of Atwood and Canada in the same critical space is not unusual.

Despite these claims, the notion of a distinct Canadian literature is still the subject of a great deal of critical debate. Sarah Corse argues that any clear distinction between Canadian literature and US literature may be a false one, and that 'national literatures exist not because they unconsciously reflect "real" national differences, but because they are integral to the process of constructing national differences' (Corse 12). In other words, there seems to be some benefit to claiming a distinction between different kinds of national literature, but this benefit may not reflect reality. Hence the list of attributes of Canadian literature noted above.

Perhaps, in literary terms, Frye was the first to rework the notion of Canadian identity when he asked a different question: not 'Who am I?' but ' "Where is here?" ' (Frye 1971, 220). Atwood herself used the familiar metaphor of literature as a mirror in her first critical book, reflecting a culture back on itself. She argues, 'If a country or a culture lacks such mirrors it has no way of knowing what it looks like; it must travel blind' (*Surv* 15–16). Thus there is a certain self-consciousness about the project of defining Canadian literature: is it a reaction to the dominance first of England and then the USA? Does it take into account the voices of multicultural writers and immigrants? Does it attempt to find a soothing consistency of theme and tone?

Robert Kroetsch's collection of essays, *The Lovely Treachery of Words*, analyses the subject from several different angles, and even invokes (as well as contests) Frye's ideas. He argues,

> The question of identity is not exactly the Canadian question. That is an interpretative matter for people who already have their story. We ask, rather, what is the narrative of us? We continue to have a crisis about our own story. The very ability to see ourselves is based on the narrative mode: the I telling a story of I, of we, of the they who mirror us. We name, from the world's story-body, the recurrences and obsessions and strategies that become, in turn, the naming of a culture called Canada.
>
> (Kroetsch 70)

In his acknowledgements, Kroetsch writes, 'I wear geography next to my skin' (ix), a powerful image that succinctly demonstrates the persuasive pull of geographical metaphors. Certainly, the landscape of Canada is a powerful image for Atwood, too, and she rarely sets her novels outside it – only in her dystopian fictions, *The Handmaid's Tale*, *Oryx and Crake* and *The Year of the Flood*, as well as her political novel, *Bodily Harm*, and even in this last novel in the list, Canada is the setting for half of it. Moreover, Atwood overtly addresses the question of creeping Americanism in *Surfacing*, one of her most widely read novels. Encountering a group of fishermen in a remote spot while searching for her missing father, the narrator and her companions assume from their behaviour and appearance that they are from the USA: 'They had a starry flag like all of them, a miniature decal sticker on the canoe bow. To show us we were in occupied territory' (*Surf* 115). Yet in this instance, they are mistaken: the men are Canadians. Atwood's narrator revises her initial assessment, but only slightly, reassigning nationality on the basis of behaviour and not passports.

As a critic, Atwood has written on nationalism, on the differences between US citizens and Canadians, and on the importance of asserting a national identity, but she is also quick to point out that her characters speak for themselves – not for her. Nevertheless, one of the important contexts for considering Atwood's work is her position as a Canadian, and her prominence in the twentieth (and twenty-first)-century canon.

In a survey conducted in 2000 for the British Association for Canadian Studies (BACS) Literature Group, published in their newsletter *CanText* and later used for part of Susan Billingham and Danielle Fuller's essay 'Can Lit(e): Fit for Export?', Atwood was revealed – unsurprisingly – as the most frequently studied Canadian author on UK university syllabi, with over twice as many books featured as her nearest rival, Michael Ondaatje, and with three times the popularity of Ondaatje when non-text specific replies were factored in. No doubt the ready availability of her books as well as the range of her writing contributed to this result, but what was also key to her popularity as a canonical author was the personal preference of the lecturers surveyed, as well as the familiarity with Atwood's work for incoming students, many of whom had read *The Handmaid's Tale* for their A Level coursework.

Significantly, in a poll of Canadian academics undertaken by *Quill and Quire* at nearly the same time, which focused on the '50 greatest 20th Century Fictional Texts by Canadians', a book by Atwood did not make the top ten.[1] This disparity in results suggests something fundamental about Atwood's reputation. One German scholar, Caroline Rosenthal, was surprised at negative or lukewarm responses to Atwood in Canada, which did not match the reactions from other parts of the world. Rosenthal concluded that Canada had a 'specific relationship to its most renowned author, who is proudly referred to as a superstar, on the one hand, and who is rejected for being one on the other' (Rosenthal 43). However, Lorraine York reminds us that 'essentialized concepts of national character offer a theoretically flawed way of accounting for the contradictions that are typical of the celebrity phenomenon' (York 118). It could simply be, as Charlotte Templin argues about Anne Tyler, that 'ranking the artistic productions of one's own countrymen and -women and evaluating their visions of one's own culture is fraught with more emotion than making evaluations of writers that represent another national literary tradition' (Templin 179). Whilst the current focus on transnationalism as a response to literary endeavour might find fault with such a pronouncement, nonetheless there is a certain measure of truth in Templin's construction: hence the less ambivalent response to Atwood's canon in the UK and elsewhere. Atwood herself, in an interview with Linda Sandler, suggests, 'The literature of one's own country is not escape literature. It tells truths, some of them hard' (Sandler in Ingersoll 31). The concept of 'truth' is also, of course, critically debated, and its status in relation to the author-as-spokesperson (as well as author-as-celebrity) is at best tricky: a phenomenon which Atwood herself addresses in both her critical and creative work.

Of course, the different cultural narratives and norms of (and within) Canada and the UK (as well as elsewhere in Europe) necessarily ensure that what Atwood 'says' is variously interpreted. For example, Atwood has been considered an 'American' writer in parts of Europe,[2] and her work has been placed in 'American Studies' modules in the UK, whereas she is explicitly situated as 'Canadian' in other contexts. Thus, Atwood is both a *cultural commentator* and a *cultural export*, and there is an acknowledged tension between these various roles. Indeed, in my interview with Atwood, she argued strongly that her role as an artist was to be a mouthpiece, principally so that the government voice was not the only one which resonated outside Canada. Commenting on the federal government's proposals to cut funding for the arts and promotion of Canadian art, Atwood was clear where she stood politically:

> Well they hate us. Basically they hate artists. There's no other explanation. Because why else would you make 600,000 mouthy enemies? That's how many people are affected by the arts or who work for the arts in Canada, and there's no reason for doing that; it's not a smart move. There's no reason other than an ideological reason: we hate artists. And 'I Stephen Harper want no voice to resound abroad except mine'.

Yann Martel makes a similar argument in his *cri de coeur* about arts funding, published on a website entitled 'What is Stephen Harper Reading' as well as in the 14 April 2007 edition of *The Globe and Mail*. Like Atwood, Martel is a successful Canadian export whose work has worldwide appeal following the publication of his award-winning novel *Life of Pi* (2001). Martel makes a provocative point about arts funding in Canada:

> Just so that you know: the parliamentary appropriation this year [2007] for the Canada Council for the Arts is $173 million. Next year it will be $182 million. Does that sound like a lot? Let me put it into perspective. A budget of $182 million translates to $5.50 per Canadian per year. Most Canadians I know spend more than that in a week on parking, some in a day on coffee.[3]

Licensed to speak by and for Canada through their very positions as exports, writers such as Martel and, more importantly, Atwood offer up *their* versions of Canada, versions potentially at odds with that the government might like to reproduce. Atwood as a 'mouthy enemy' is a force to be reckoned with, given her global sales, her status as a politically engaged and intellectual writer, and her popularity with a range of readers. Indeed, in 1997, in a postmodern twist on the packaging of an author, her face was superimposed on the plastic bags that Barnes & Noble used to sell their books (York 102), a decision taken by a large American company precisely to increase sales. Atwood sells – and sells well – and the commercial aspect of celebrity cannot be overestimated. Moreover, the very fact that Atwood can package and sell her collected book reviews and occasional writing – work that is really only of interest because of its connection to Atwood-as-author – suggests just how much force she has in the literary (and business) world.

Atwood's criticism: amateur plumbing

Atwood playfully suggests, 'As a theorist, I'm a good amateur plumber. You do what you have to do to keep your sink from overflowing' (Hancock in Ingersoll 108). Atwood's flippant modesty aside, it is clear that she has had a significant influence on the reception of Canadian literature and criticism. Atwood is the author of six collections of literary/cultural criticism, as well as other non-fiction work (including, for example, a short illustrated history of Canada, *Days of the Rebels 1815–1840*, in 1977, and *Two Solicitudes: Conversations*, based on interviews with Victor-Lévy Beaulieu), and from the first, her critical stance has been seen as controversial.

Atwood's approach to criticism is open-ended, 'playfully amateur' yet at the same time acutely analytical. As Walter Pache notes, 'Atwood does not conceive of the critic as the reader's antagonist or as a legislator who lays down the laws for a "correct" textual analysis, but rather sees herself as a guide helping her readers into the text, stimulating them to follow their own instinct and use their own imagination' (Pache in Nischik 128). She also believes in transparency, and avoiding jargon; for Atwood, criticism needs to be 'graspable' (Hancock in Ingersoll 108).

Atwood's first foray into criticism, *Survival: A Thematic Guide to Canadian Literature* (1972), was controversial from the start, and its impact is still felt on Canadian letters. Indeed, Sharon Rose Wilson argues that *Survival* 'may even have helped precipitate a literary shift away from its central premise' (Wilson xiii), otherwise known as Atwood's 'victim theory'. *Survival* was published as a moneymaker for the House of Anansi Press, and it adopted a journalistic approach rather than that of a 'professional critic' (much like Germaine Greer's *The Female Eunuch*). Also like Greer's text, it has become a seminal text and is reviewed in a different light from its original 'intention'. It was and continues to be roundly attacked by critics – whom Atwood refers to as 'the footnote crowd' (*SW* 105) – but many general readers appear to find some helpful directions in it. Whilst critics found it reductive and brash, and disliked what was perceived as Atwood's flippancy, a number of her ideas have found their way into general parlance.

The key point of the book is that it situates Canadian literature in its own space and explores what Atwood sees as Canadian literature's patterns and motifs. It is unashamedly 'thematic' criticism (as the title denotes), a form of criticism that does have its detractors. The problem with thematic criticism, according to Francesco Loriggio, is its insistence on coherence, an imagined linkage which becomes a unitary whole (59). Thus, whatever fits a critic's scheme is included, but whatever does not is abandoned, and as a result, such criticism might tell you more about the way that a particular critic's mind works than the way a whole canon of literature works, because of the pre-selection involved.

Atwood acknowledges that the book is neither exhaustive nor evaluative (points with which a number of critics have taken issue, so much so that Atwood felt obliged to respond in writing to at least one critic, Robin Mathews, in an essay found in her second collection of literary and cultural criticism, *Second Words*). *Survival* also moves beyond a sort of national stereotype of pointing out shortcomings; in fact, Atwood points to Canadian literature's many strengths. It blends, as well, 'textual analysis, literary history and political assessment' (Pache in Nischik 123). Atwood has subsequently suggested that the book offered a 'working hypothesis, to be altered or discarded if one more in accord with literary reality comes along. It should be regarded as a stage in a dialogue' (*SW* 134). The book is divided into twelve chapters, addressing a range of themes including animals, monstrous nature, death, paralysed artists and women, amongst others. Her main thesis, as the title suggests, is that Canadian literature is primarily related to survival.

One crucial element of the book is Atwood's elaboration on what she calls 'basic victim positions'. The four stages or positions are first, denial of victimhood; then acknowledgement of victimhood but suggesting that this is the fault of someone or something else, such as fate, biology, God, history or the unconscious; third, acknowledgement of victimhood but refusing to accept the position as inevitable, and finally, creative non-victimhood (*Surv* 36–8). In this final position, 'Victor/Victim games are obsolete' (*Surv* 39). In the moment of writing, Atwood suggests that the author attains position four, though the text itself may be trapped in one of the earlier positions (*Surv* 40).

It has been argued that Atwood has applied her own theories to her creative work, or has extrapolated from her own work outwards. It is certainly the case, for example, that there are resonances between *Surfacing* and *Survival*, both published the same year, though Atwood denies that one was written to validate the other. Nevertheless, there are instructive comparisons to be made between the texts, from the Rapunzel syndrome (*Surv* 209) she identifies, where the enclosed woman is unable to communicate well, to the rescuer who turns out to be not much help; the narrator's boyfriend communicates as poorly as she does. Atwood also argues that a 'magic baby' motif crops up frequently in Canadian novels, and it is certainly the case that the novel ends with a potential baby as a rescuing fantasy. Atwood also outlines the importance of the presence of 'failed' or 'mediocre' artists (*Surv* 136) as well as archaeological motifs in Canadian fiction, both of which are key aspects of *Surfacing*. The narrator is a commercial artist who has learned to 'imitate anything' (*Surf* 47) and who compromises on her illustrations before submitting them, in order to fend off criticism, and her boyfriend teaches adult education but 'mangles' pots as a sign of his artistic superiority (*Surf* 51). There's more than a hint of the old adage, 'Those who can, do; those who can't, teach' in Atwood's assignment of a teaching role to Joe. Moreover, the narrator's father is seeking archaeological information when he disappears. It is, however, the victim positions that Atwood outlines in *Survival* that most connect with *Surfacing*, and readers must decide whether the narrator is able to achieve the position of 'creative non-victim' in the end and whether any of the other characters move beyond their victim status.

Pache argues that Atwood's critical work was influenced strongly by two critics, the first of whom was Northrop Frye, with whom Atwood studied at the University of Toronto. Pache notes Frye's influences in relation to his methodologies, wide range of references and his construction of the 'garrison mentality'. The second influential critic was Robert Graves, author of *The White Goddess* (1948), which Atwood mines in her creative work as well (Pache in Nischik 122). In her poetry as well as her fiction, Atwood returns, for example, to Graves' idea of the triple goddess.

In 1982, Atwood published *Second Words*, which collected together fifty essays ranging from reviews and introductions to other people's books to essays on what it is like to be a woman writer ('On Being a Woman Writer', 'The Curse of Eve – or What I Learned in School', 'Witches'), the politics of literature ('An End to Audience?', 'Writing the Male Character'), essays on her own literature ('Mathews and Misrepresentation', 'An Introduction to *The Edible Woman*') or US-Canadian relations ('Nationalism, Limbo and the Canadian Club', 'Canadian-American Relations: Surviving the Eighties'). Of course, several pieces straddle these categories, too. Though some pieces pre-date *Survival*, we see an amazing range of texts, and an indication of Atwood's enjoying a high regard in media terms, given the number of reviews she is asked to undertake. As the same time, this collection moves beyond Canadian literature quite significantly. If there is a connecting issue here, Pache suggests that it is 'the social responsibility of the writer, and also a deep commitment to criticism as a vital human activity, which is nonetheless of secondary importance to the creative writer' (Pache in Nischik 124).

This collection was followed by *Strange Things: The Malevolent North in Canadian Fiction* (1995), a series of four essays on the North, ranging from an exploration of Sir John Franklin's search for the North-west Passage, to an analysis of Grey Owl, a discussion of the mythical wendigo (a Canadian monster who resembles a werewolf and is known to cannibalize its own family), and the wilderness in women's literature. Atwood's focus is ecological in these essays, as she grapples with the meaning of the north (and touches on her familiar territory, survival).

Atwood was asked to give the Empson Lectures in 2000, and *Negotiating with the Dead* (2002) is a reworking of her six lectures into an essay format. They take the following metaphors as chapter titles: 'Orientation'; 'Duplicity'; 'Dedication'; 'Temptation'; 'Communion' and 'Descent'. In these essays, Atwood explores what writing means (for herself and others) and what roles individual authors are seen to undertake. This is perhaps her most sophisticated critical undertaking, blending autobiographical snippets with a display of her wide-ranging reading. Atwood seeks to explore the doubleness of the writer, and where writing comes from. She argues that the writer is inevitably doubled, because the writer is both 'the person who exists when no writing is going forward' and 'that other, more shadowy and altogether more equivocal personage who shares the same body, and who, when no one is looking, takes it over and uses it to commit the actual writing' (*ND* 35). Atwood uses the doubled artist in several ways in her own work, from Joan's 'automatic' writing in *Lady Oracle*, undertaken in a trance-like state, to Elaine Risley's visual art in *Cat's Eye*, which is only partially understood by the artist herself, to the exploration of the doubleness of the writer in *The Blind Assassin*, where Iris is seen as her sister Laura's 'odd, extra hand, attached to no body – the hand that passed her on, to the world, to them' (*BA* 287). Atwood also focuses on the image of hands, 'Dexter and sinister' (*ND* 37), an image that recurs in *Bodily Harm*, where hands are misplaced and unrecognized, as well as in her poetry. Atwood's essays then address the thorny issue of money, eschewing the notion that writers write for the love of writing alone, and she looks, too, at the many myths of the female writer, a recurring topic in her work (and explored further below). This collection is a remarkable companion to Atwood's own work, and offers the reader a glimpse at her critical frameworks.

Atwood published *Curious Pursuits: Occasional Writing* in the UK in 2005, a collection of thirty-five years of writing from 1970 to 2005.[4] This collection includes forty-seven pieces ranging from reviews and other pieces published in newspapers and magazines (including obituaries) to responses to world politics and analyses of her own writing experiences. 'Nine Beginnings', for example, offers nine different answers to the question 'Why do you write?', none of them definitive. Atwood includes a piece addressed to America, post 9/11, a short essay on 'Writing *Oryx and Crake*' and an essay on rereading Virginia Woolf's *To the Lighthouse*. In the collection, Atwood plays around with her own interests, hoping that they will interest others. In exploring her title, *Curious Pursuits*, for example, Atwood notes:

> 'Curious' describes both my habitual state of mind – a less kind word would be 'nosy' – as well as the subject matter of some of these writings. Like Alice, I've become curiouser and curiouser myself, and the world

has done the same. Another way of putting it: if something doesn't arouse my curiosity, I'm not likely to write about it. Though perhaps 'curious' as a word carries too light a weight: my curiosities are (I hope) not idle ones. 'Passionate' might have been more accurate; however, it would have given a wrong impression, and disappointed a few men in raincoats.   (*CP* xv)

For the purposes of exploring Atwood's fiction further, there are two essays in the collection that warrant deeper analysis. 'Spotty-Handed Villain-esses: The Problem of Female Bad Behaviour in the Creation of Literature' and 'In Search of *Alias Grace*: On Writing Canadian Historical Fiction' both reveal important contexts for her work. The first of these, 'Spotty-Handed Villainesses', challenges the assumption that female characters must be good to be feminist. As Atwood claims, 'Create a flawless character and you create an insufferable one; which may be why I am interested in spots' (*CP* 172). Atwood has made many a foray into the realm of females' bad behaviour, from *Cat's Eye*, where girls' plots against each other almost have a fatal end, to *The Robber Bride*, where Zenia plots against women by stealing (and using up) their men; to *Alias Grace*, where Grace argues that if people 'want a monster so badly they ought to be provided with one' (*AG* 33). Provide one she does, exhibiting behaviour that is considered 'mad' on more than one occasion. Moreover, Grace contemplates madness as a role:

> I think of all the things that have been written about me – that I am an inhuman female demon, that I am an innocent victim of a blackguard forced against my will and in danger of my own life, that I was too ignorant to know how to act and that to hang me would be judicial murder, that I am fond of animals, that I am very handsome with a brilliant complexion, that I have blue eyes, that I have green eyes, that I have auburn and also brown hair, that I am tall and also not above the average height, that I am well and decently dressed, that I robbed a dead woman to appear so, that I am brisk and smart about my work, that I am of a sullen disposition with a quarrelsome temper, that I have the appearance of a person rather above my humble station, that I am a good girl with a pliable nature and no harm is told of me, that I am cunning and devious, that I am soft in the head and little better than an idiot. And I wonder, how can I be all of these different things at once?
>
> (*AG* 23)

Atwood asks, rhetorically, why men should get all the 'juicy parts' (*CP* 181) and why women should be homogenized as good, or simply as victims. Atwood calls on women characters, 'Take back the night! In particular, take back The Queen of the Night, from Mozart's *Magic Flute*. It's a great part, and due for revision' (*CP* 181). Here, Atwood uses the words of feminism ('Take Back the Night' being a campaign for women's safety) and offers up a parallel scenario. She suggests that women's very real political oppression should not limit fictional women's behaviour boundaries. Atwood suggests that 'female bad characters can also act as keys to doors we need to open, and as mirrors in which we can see more than just a pretty face' (*CP* 182). Atwood even unpicks the apparent goodness of Penelope in *The Penelopiad*, making her a far richer character than literary history has previously assumed. Thus, 'Spotty-Handed Villainnesses' offers a way of reading a number of Atwood's texts, uncovering her motives for exploring the darker side of female (human) nature.

In her essay 'In Search of *Alias Grace*: On Writing Canadian Historical Fiction', Atwood explores further the genesis of her novel, but also ranges beyond it, and some of her ideas can be applied to her other texts. For example, in exploring memory, Atwood claims, 'As a rule, we tend to remember the awful things done to us, and to forget the awful things we did' (*CP* 212), yet her subsequent novel *The Blind Assassin* attempts to tackle both (revealing, yet again, another woman behaving badly). In this essay Atwood returns to the notion that her generation of writers had grown up with the 'illusion' that there was no Canadian literature, and so they set about creating it. She also claims that 'history, for us, either didn't exist, or it had happened elsewhere, or if ours it was boring' (*CP* 217), thus an insistent focus on the contemporary in the writing of their apprenticeships. Atwood suggests that a turn to historical musings happened first in poetry, and references her own *The Journals of Susanna Moodie* (*CP* 218); she also explores why the historical novel gained popularity in the last twenty years of the twentieth century. She suggests, 'by taking a long hard look backwards, we place ourselves' (*CP* 223). The essay concludes with an analysis of how she wrote *Alias Grace*, and the rules she offered to herself when writing such historical fiction, including the fact that she stayed faithful to what was in the public domain, whilst in the gaps, she felt 'free to invent' (*CP* 227). Hence the discontinuities about Grace noted above. Atwood argues at the end of the essay, 'The past belongs to us, because we are the ones who need it' (*CP* 229). Atwood's own criticism thus offers up avenues for exploring not only her texts, but others as well.

Atwood's most recent collection is *Payback: Debt as Metaphor and the Shadow Side of Wealth* (2008), a text which seemed somewhat prescient given the worldwide recession that followed shortly after publication. *Payback* begins with a historical assessment of debt, 'Ancient Balances', which explores the femaleness of Justice as a figure, followed by 'Debt and Sin', that examines not only Christianity, but other explanations for behaviour. In this chapter, Atwood analyses the figure of the Sin Eater, which she has also used in a short story of the same name, collected in *Dancing Girls* in the UK and in *Bluebeard's Egg* in North America, as well as the image of sacrificial victims, which are part of the inner story of *The Blind Assassin*. In 'Debt as Plot', Atwood turns to a number of fictional texts, including novels by Dickens, Eliot and Thackeray, and to plays such as *Dr Faustus*, and in 'Shadow' turns to Shakespeare, exploring *The Merchant of Venice*, and returns to Dickens. The book concludes with the title essay, 'Payback'. In this essay, she images Ebenezer Scrooge as 'Scrooge Nouveau', a corporate businessman; the Spirit of Earth Day Past takes him through the ages and instructs him that in a global crisis, there are only limited options: 'Protect Yourself, Give Up and Party, Help Others, Blame, Bear Witness, and Go About Your Life'; in war, two other options, 'Fight, and Surrender' also offer themselves up (*PB* 186). Atwood's allegory is distinctly ecological, with the future of the planet hanging in the balance. Atwood argues that a revision of what constitutes wealth and debt is required in order to drive us away from the course towards destruction.

The book began life as the Massey Lectures and thus follows a familiar pattern. Atwood's critical works begin in one format – often as speeches or lectures – and become transformed from time-bound and singular pieces into ones that can be perused and mined again and again. They also offer a sense of context not only for Atwood's writing, but for her reading and world view, as well.

On being a woman writer, writing about women

Irvine also suggests that Canadian literature benefits from the 'seriousness with which it treats women's quests' (Irvine in Davison and Broner 243). These elements are clearly at work in Atwood's novels, poetry and short stories, in obvious ways in novels such as *Surfacing* as well as in more subtle ways in a number of her poems. Indeed, it is impossible to consider Atwood's work without considering the central importance she places on women as characters, with every one of her novels, except *Oryx and Crake*, featuring a female protagonist, and most of her short stories doing so as well. Atwood's investigation of female subjectivity ranges from explorations of the female as victim, to representations of the dissembling, monstrous female. Throughout her writing, she reinvents the subject of 'woman', while also acknowledging the need to 'take the capital W off Woman' (*SW* 227).

In an interview with Geoff Hancock, Atwood returns to the idea of Woman: 'As for woman, capital W, we got stuck with that for centuries. Eternal woman. But really, 'Woman' is the sum total of women. It doesn't exist apart from that, except as an abstracted idea' (Hancock in Ingersoll 101). Atwood's stance, then, is one whereby she focuses primarily on the female because it is the female's position that she knows best, but she does not assume that this is a singular position, anymore than she suggests that all men think alike. Women deserve equality under the law, Atwood has argued, but it does not mean that women and men are the same.

One of the key questions for any exploration of Atwood and her work is the extent to which she can be considered a feminist writer, despite her refusal to align herself publicly with the movement. Indeed, the majority of the criticism on Atwood's oeuvre is decidedly feminist, which means that critics must grapple with the fact that so many of her characters spout anti-feminist sentiments – whilst clearly being entrapped in a patriarchal framework that cries out for a feminist interpretation.

Atwood explains her position in a number of different ways. In her 1976 essay 'On Being a "Woman Writer"' (collected in *Second Words*), she argues that she is a writer who has been more adopted by the women's movement than a particular member herself. She began writing at a time when the second wave women's movement was not visible (though her first novel coincided with its public rise). When she did write, she claims, she was like many other women writers, having to

> defy other women's as well as men's ideas of what was proper, and it's not finally all that comforting to have a phalanx of women – some younger and relatively unscathed, others from their own generation, the bunch that was collecting china, changing diapers and sneering at any female with intellectual pretensions 20 or even 10 years ago [that is, between 1956–66] come breezing up now to tell them they were right all along.   (*SW* 191)

Yet she also believes that the period between the mid-1970s and 1980s offered women the chance to 'say things that once you couldn't say. And therefore, being able to see things that once you couldn't see, or that you would have seen but repressed, or that you would have seen and put another interpretation on …' (Castro in Van Spanckeren and Castro 231). In fact, a great number of Atwood's heroines are trapped in perspectives that do not make sense until they adopt a feminist sensibility – though they may never come to that conclusion themselves, being trapped in a viewpoint that does not expand outward.

In numerous interviews, Atwood has reiterated her views that novels are not political tracts and that she is under no obligation to toe a party line – or to be a role model. She dislikes rigid ideology. She is also concerned that a strict allegiance to a cause will damage her writing. She is, she argues, not a propagandist but an observer; her work merely reflects the reality of an uneven distribution of power between men and women. She certainly writes against the grain, which is a key element of much feminist criticism that seeks to denaturalize the seemingly natural. She even explores the limits of feminism as a political force; in *The Handmaid's Tale*, Offred's mother is a radical feminist who raised Offred on her own, took her to political rallies (including, at one point, a rally at which pornography was burned), and longed for a woman's world. Offred is living within a 'woman's world' in her segregated society and imagines a conversation with her mother: 'Mother, I think. Wherever you may be. Can you hear me? You wanted a women's culture. Well, now there is one. It isn't what you mean, but it exists. Be thankful for small mercies' (*HT* 137). As Atwood reveals, a women's culture does not necessarily mean that the culture will be better than what went before – separatism of any kind is suspect, and feminism itself requires careful surveillance, too.

At the same time, Atwood has herself set out to enumerate the benefits of feminism to literature: 'the expansion of the territory available to writers, both in character and in language; a sharp-eyed examination of the way power works in gender relations, and the exposure of much of this as socially constructed; a vigorous exploration of many hitherto-concealed areas of experience' (*CP* 179). Atwood also recognizes that women's writing is reviewed differently from men's writing, and that she cannot divorce the two identities – woman, writer – completely. Atwood argues, 'As writers, women writers are like other writers', but 'As biological specimens and as citizens … women are like other women: subject to the same discriminatory laws, encountering the same demeaning attitudes, burdened with the same good reasons for not walking through the park alone after dark. They too have bodies' (*SW* 194).

Atwood has been known to become exasperated in interviews or at book readings by being asked whether she is a feminist. A number of her critical texts skirt around the issue, including *Negotiating with the Dead*, in which she asks (but does not answer) the question, 'If you're a woman and a writer, does that combination of gender and vocation automatically make you a feminist, and what does that mean, exactly?' (*ND* 106). Perhaps it means whatever the critic thinks it does, but readers of Atwood's work must take care when ascribing political views to her, or assuming that the stances adopted by her characters equate with her own. Nevertheless, the question of feminism cannot be set aside – as is clear in the next chapter, where her work is surveyed and explored with feminist readings clearly in mind.

Chapter 3

Works

Atwood is the author of over thirty-five books, ranging from novels to poetry, short story collections, books of essays and books that defy easy classification (in lists on the inside of her books, Atwood tends to classify them under the wider category of 'fiction'). Atwood is also the author of six children's books, from her first, *Up in the Tree* (1978) to *Bashful Bob and Doleful Dorinda* (2004) and her visual art and photography have been used in her own books as well as in books about her. Atwood welcomes the challenges of genre writing but always infuses those genres with a political slant that offsets the 'conventions' and boundaries that the genres initially suggest. Several images and ideas recur throughout her oeuvre, across genres; she experiments with a range of styles; and she challenges readers with her comic wit as well as her fierce intelligence. She is thus an author with a wide range of outputs that offer a number of avenues for exploration. In what follows I will aim to give an overview of her main outputs, exploring first her novels, then her short story collections, before finishing with her poetry. Her children's books are relatively unexplored critically and rarely feature on course syllabi; as a result, I have taken the decision to exclude them from sustained analysis here.

Novels

For Atwood, writing novels is hard work: 'If you write a novel, you know that you're going to be writing very hard for a minimum of a year and a half. You know you're going to get pains in your arms. You know you're going to get pains in your neck. You know you're going to get headaches. It is hard, physical work' (Ingersoll 262). Luckily for the reading world, Atwood is willing to put up with the pain and has produced twelve novels, from her first, *The Edible*

Woman, published in 1969, to her latest, *The Year of the Flood*, published in 2009.

The Edible Woman sets up the conflict between self and other that most of her other novels explore even further. The central protagonist, Marian MacAlpin, becomes a sort of Alice-in-Wonderland figure, who has a number of disconcerting experiences. The novel moves from first-person to third-person narration, a change that coincides with Marian's loss of a sense of identity. It is clear that in her society, she is expected to take on roles (fiancée, wife) rather than maintain her ego-boundaries. It is tempting to link Atwood's novel to the women's movement of the late 1960s and 1970s, particularly to Betty Friedan's ground-breaking text *The Feminine Mystique*, which identified what she called the 'problem with no name' – a sense of unease when the basic needs of life were fulfilled, but a woman still felt unhappy, uneasy, unrewarded. Friedan argues that '[t]he feminine mystique says that the highest value and the only commitment for women is the fulfilment of their own femininity' (38), and that it 'permits, even encourages, women to ignore the question of their identity' (63), which could be seen as a gloss on Atwood's text itself. Yet when asked about this remarkably prescient book, Atwood noted:

> Actually, the timing of *The Edible Woman* was kind of an accident. I actually wrote it in '64–'65 and Jack McClelland lost the manuscript, although that's not his story. He said somebody else lost it. It wasn't around for a while, let's put it that way. I was so busy passing my orals that I didn't have a lot of time to think about it. So it actually came out in 69 and it *was* strange timing. It was right on the edge, so much so that there were basically two kinds of reviews. The ones that didn't know feminism had arrived said, 'This is a novel by a very young writer, but she will become more mature and take a more balanced view of things later'! The critics that did know about feminism responded accordingly. It was quite an interesting experience being there at that time, because you got all the hysterical reactions to feminism dumped right on you or, to be more accurate, I got them dumped on me. For example the stringer from *Time* was asking questions like, 'Do men like you?' My response: 'Well honey, it depends *which* men, doesn't it?' Sometimes they asked, 'Do you like men?' Same answer.[1]

Here, Atwood's well-known humour asserts itself and in her disavowal of an overt feminist consciousness, Atwood maintains her stance that literature and political tracts are separate. At the same time, though, Atwood recognizes that a writer cannot help but be part of her historical time, and in writing this novel, it is clear that Atwood is reflecting on the situation of educated women whose life choices seemed limited in the 1960s.

Marian, for example, lives with her flatmate Ainsley Tewce, and both of them, though university graduates, have jobs that do not make full use of their talents: Ainsley is a tester of defective electric toothbrushes and Marian works for Seymour Surveys in low-level market research. In fact, she works in what she calls the 'gooey layer' (*EW* 19) in the middle of the hierarchical institution, between the top layer, the male executives and male psychologists, and the bottom layer, the machinery. She rewrites questionnaires so that they are appealing to the housewives they target, and sometimes ends up conducting surveys herself. On one such jaunt, she meets up with the ethereal Duncan and his roommates Trevor and Fish, characters who lend a certain unreality to the text. In fact, references to unreality, the make-believe and fairy tales litter the novel in relation to Duncan in particular, who may or may not be real; this insertion of potentially unreal characters is also explored by Atwood in later novels such as *The Robber Bride* (which also signals its relationship to fairy tales).

Here, Duncan acts as a foil for Marian, expressing her inexpressible desires. He fails to act as required by society. He lies for no apparent reason and is fully engaged only with himself. All of these are aspects of identity that Marian tries to set aside, maintaining instead a sense that she is respectable – that she is what others want her to be, from a good lodger for the 'lady downstairs' who owns the house she lives in, to a good worker, a good girlfriend (one who does not make claims) and a good citizen. Early in the novel, Marian is pressed to join the pension plan at work and worries, 'Somewhere in front of me was a self waiting, pre-formed, a self who had worked during innumerable years for Seymour Surveys and was now receiving her reward. A pension. I foresaw a bleak room with a plug-in electric heater' (*EW* 21).

Partly to avoid this fate, and partly accidentally, Marian agrees to marry her boyfriend Peter, a decision that means not only will she *not* have to take up the pension option, but she will no longer be able to remain working for the company, as women were generally expected to leave their employment upon marriage (a historical reality that readers must confront in reading this novel some 40 years after it was published). Marian has no strong views about marriage, simply assuming that it will be part of her future. Unlike her, Ainsley is against marriage, and she represents – at least at first – a radical alternative. Ainsley tricks Peter's friend Len into impregnating her, intending to become a single mother – a brave (and societally unacceptable) choice in the 1960s. However, later in the text, convinced by false psychology that if her child is a boy, and growing up alone with her, he will become homosexual, Ainsley ends up 'choosing' the traditional fate of marriage after all (though to someone else entirely). Indeed, she even ends up going to Niagara Falls for a stereotypical honeymoon, though with her less-than-stereotypical new husband, Fish.

In part two of the book, after agreeing to get married, Marian loses her first-person voice – and her appetite. Atwood perceptively links Marian's sense of identity with the space that she is allowed to take up: a space that shrinks as she becomes fiancée rather than woman. It is particularly significant that Atwood earlier linked Marian directly to hunger and food, with many passages focusing on eating. As Margaret Griffith perceptively notes, Marian 'gradually withdraws from her role in the consumer plot by refusing to eat' (Griffith 87). Not all critics have seen the intricacies of Atwood's plot, however, and it is intriguing to explore the reactions of early male critics to the text. George Woodcock, for example, a very well-known and respected critic of Canadian literature, argued that, rather than being a victim in this marriage plot, Marian has 'cannibalistically, trapped a highly normal young man into a proposal of marriage' (Woodcock 93). The choice of words itself is intriguing, given her inability to eat during this period in the novel. Similarly, T. D. MacLulich summed up the text thus: 'In short, Marian fears destruction by sex. Why does Marian view sex in such an abnormal way?' (MacLulich 188). What Marian actually fears – but cannot articulate – is the loss of herself that her new role – a role which would displace and indeed cancel all previous roles – seems to ensure. The role of wife, and not the role of sexual partner, is the role which causes so much trepidation (after all, Marian is not, as the novel makes very clear, destined to be a virginal bride).

In these readings, Peter is normal and Marian is abnormal; yet it is clear now, with the benefit of feminist analysis, that what may appear to be 'normal' is anything but. Although Marian is, for example, depicted as finding children disgusting when visiting her pregnant friend Clara, again this disgust is principally because of Clara's surroundings and the fear that maternity can only be read as monstrous. In this way, she sees Clara as a reflection of her future, and it is not an entirely agreeable one. MacLulich argues that in refusing food, Marian uses the only weapon a child has. But Marian is not, of course, a child, except if one considers the position that her society seems to want her to fulfil. Marian's refusal to eat may be a cry for help, but it is a cry more that she herself needs to recognize than anyone outside her needs to hear. Indeed, it does not manifest itself into 'real' anorexia (a disease, in 1969, without the high profile it has today) but is, rather, a symbolic gesture of refusal to conform, even whilst apparently doing so.

Similarly, Atwood uses the character Duncan as a sort of alter ego for Marian and even Peter, disrupting the romance plot. Marian claims about Duncan, 'The extent to which he could ignore her point of view was amazing' (*EW* 189), yet this is exactly what both Peter and Marian do once they are engaged (and even before). Duncan acts out what Marian is feeling, though it takes her until the end of the novel to see it.

What some early critics found difficult to deal with was a new world view in which educated women did not automatically take mediocre jobs and wait around to get married. Atwood seems to tap into that mood very early on; moreover, she taps into the unresolved tension between feminism and femininity. As J. Brooks Bouson argues, all of 'Atwood's novels emphasize women's consent to femininity, and they also, in their relentless focus on the female experience of self, dramatize the vulnerable selfhood of women' (Bouson 1993, 10), and never is this clearer than in this first published novel. Indeed, it is not accidental that the moment Marian gets engaged, she becomes trapped in a repetition of beauty treatments that make her over, or unmake her. At a beauty salon in preparation for a party, Marian perceptively notes, 'They treated your head like a cake: something to be carefully iced and ornamented' (*EW* 208). Here, Atwood carefully combines the image of artifice – femininity is not innate but made – and food, setting up the reader for the final image of the edible woman that will come at the end of Part Two of the novel. When Duncan arrives at a party she is hosting (and for which she has remade herself in an image of feminine beauty), he says, 'You didn't tell me it was a masquerade … Who the hell are you supposed to be?' (*EW* 239).

The question resonates, and not surprisingly, it finally allows Marian to see what she has bought into. To unmake herself, she runs away, attempts to engage in a sexual relationship with Duncan and returns home. Then, she lovingly bakes a cake in the shape of a woman, which she offers up to her fiancé as a sugary substitute for herself. He is horrified and leaves abruptly, and Ainsley, returning with Fish, is similarly discombobulated by the symbol. Ainsley goes so far as to argue that, in eating the cake herself, Marian is rejecting her femininity, but here, Marian simply shrugs and replies, 'Nonsense … It's only a cake' (*EW* 273).

A short Part Three closes the novel and the novel reverts to first-person narration, and Marian tidies up her flat, focusing on what her future might hold. She is so much more herself that she is able to put even Duncan in his place. When he complains that he does not know what to do now that Fish has left with Ainsley, Marian muses, 'Now that I was thinking of myself in the first person singular again I found my own situation much more interesting than his' (*EW* 278). Nevertheless, the novel ends with Duncan voraciously consuming the edible woman. Critics are divided about this final image, and Atwood herself has noted that Marian is really no better off now than she was before: her prospects are limited, and she has, even if metaphorically, offered herself up to be consumed.

What this novel does, however, is to set up a number of recurring themes and images that Atwood will continue to explore in her fiction. As Alice Palumbo argues,

> In her novels, Atwood has made constant use of the double voice, depicting characters at war with themselves and their environments. Through intertextual allusions, alterations in narrative point of view, and the use of the unconscious, Atwood shows the way in which the self is constructed from contradictory impulses, some more societally acceptable than others. (Palumbo in Nischik 73)

These contradictions are skilfully represented, as Atwood continues to explore women's lives in comic ways as well as serious ones, acknowledging that she does not necessarily have the answers, but can at least home in on the questions that women are asking. Roberta White argues that in the first three of her novels, Atwood focuses on change and escape, as well as rescue narratives, whereby women are saved from the marriage plot and put 'in motion in stories of their own devising' (White in Pearlman 54). The idea of putting in motion – rather than completing – their stories is of paramount importance here, as Atwood's women are in the process of becoming, rather than finalizing, a series of identities – through masquerade, role-play and experimentation.

Atwood's exploration of role-play becomes even more pronounced in *Surfacing* (1972), in which the unnamed protagonist shrugs off human identity altogether by the end of the novel, preferring to seek the resolution to her problems by refusing to speak altogether. This is the novel that really established Atwood's fictional voice and reputation.

The novel begins as the narrator, a commercial artist, returns to the isolated island on which her family lived in the summers of her youth in order to look for her missing father, a 'voluntary recluse' (*Surf* 5) who has lived on his own since the death of her mother some years before. Unlike Marian, this female character does not signal her sense of self through her use of first-person narration; she does not even have a name. She is, rather, cut off from her feelings and the people around her, estranged from everyone, though this only becomes apparent slowly, since the reader initially trusts her (and indeed does not notice her lack of a name for some time).

The reader learns that the woman is travelling with her boyfriend Joe, her best friend Anna, and Anna's husband David. The original plan had been to come to look for the narrator's father and leave relatively quickly – the narrator did not even plan to see her father if he had returned – but instead the two couples agree to spend two nights in the family cabin on the lake. This later extends to a week as the men decide to fish and get away from it all. These seven days are metaphorically significant, in that the narrator's world isn't created, but essentially dismantled, during the week. Once the decision to extend is made (by the men, solely), the narrator – having come across drawings her father has done – is convinced that he has gone mad, and worries that they are targets as a result. Indeed, though not named as such, the father figure becomes, in her imagination, a sort of wendigo figure, or mythical creature who is said to watch and feed on family. With a carefully plotted symmetry, Joe and David metaphorically seem to feed on those around them, particularly in relation to the amateur film they are making, *Random Samples*. This film is made up of shots of tourist spots, which are ironically filmed; shots of a dead heron strung up as if on a crucifix (left, they think, by invasive American fishermen), and the exploitation of Anna, who is, at one point, forced to strip for the camera. At a higher level of metaphor, those who are destructive become, in the narrator's mind, Americans. All that is bad is ejected from the narrator and assigned to this other nationality – so much so that the narrator ends up assigning the category American even to those who insist they are Canadian:

> It doesn't matter what country they're from, my head said, they're still Americans, they're what's in store for us, what we're turning into. They spread themselves like a virus, they get into the brain and take over the cells and the cells change from inside and the ones that have the disease can't tell the difference. Like the late show sci-fi movies, creatures from outer space, body snatchers injecting themselves into you dispossessing your brain, their eyes blank eggshells behind the dark glasses. If you look like them and talk like them and think like them then you are them, I was saying, you speak their language, a language is everything you do. (*Surf* 123)

Atwood's focus on language in *Surfacing* has been explored critically from as early as 1976, when Nancy Bjerring published an article in the *Queen's Quarterly*; and a focus on language works well, despite the silent nature of the narrator and her inability to communicate.

For example, although the narrator calls Anna her 'best friend', the fact is that they have known each other for only two months, and no close bonds are evident: 'My friends' pasts are vague to me and to each other also, any one of us could have amnesia for years and the others wouldn't notice' (*Surf* 24). Indeed, it is telling that she is somewhat embarrassed by the fact that the disappearance of her surviving parent unsettles her, even though she has not seen him for nine years. As she records for the reader, she had thought, 'All I would have to do was come back when I was ready but I kept putting it off, there would be too many explanations' (*Surf* 3), and now it is too late. These explanations are, nevertheless, meted out carefully and unemotionally; the reader learns of a marriage and a divorce, as well as an abandoned child – factors she feels her parents would not understand. She suggests that part of her is missing: 'A divorce is like an amputation, you survive but there's less of you' (*Surf* 36). Tellingly, she later remarks that she feels she is a woman cut into two pieces: 'I was the wrong half, detached, terminal. I was nothing but a head, or no, something minor like a severed thumb; numb' (*Surf* 102).

This image of the narrator cut in half offers an important visual image, in that she is not only partial, but in a sense doubled, too. The novel suggests that the narrator's life has been split into two – before and after her apparently disastrous marriage. Yet this is not the only split she feels: she also feels that she was split as a child between the city and the bush, or, as she says, 'two anonymities' (53). Anna suggests that the narrator has a twin, because when she reads her palm she finds that 'some of your lines are double' (*Surf* 2).

It is important to recognize the way in which duplicity is threaded through the narrative, in for example, the way in which all of the characters relate to each other. One example focuses on Anna, who expresses her duplicity through her relationship with her husband. She and David present – at first – the image of a loving couple who work hard at their marriage. They 'tease' each other frequently, which the narrator first reads as a sign of their closeness and only later recognizes as passively aggressive behaviour. She gets up early to put on make-up, noting that her husband does not like to see her without it – but she subsequently claims that he does not know she wears it. The narrator notes, 'I glimpse the subterfuge this must involve, or is it devotion' (*Surf* 38). It is significant that the first word – subterfuge – is the accurate one, but that it is replaced by the more positive reading associated with the word 'devotion'. The reader understands – if the narrator does not – that subterfuge better characterizes their fraught relationship, yet it is also telling that the narrator *consciously* reworks the words she uses. This suggests that she is actively trying to change the picture. Anna claims that her marriage works because she made an 'emotional commitment' (*Surf* 41), though later that commitment is revealed as one of hate.

Although Anna is represented as deluded in her marriage, in fact, she faces reality more than the narrator. Looking at the paintings of princesses that the narrator is working on, she says, 'They shouldn't let kids have stuff like that' (*Surf* 52) since she knows the lie of happily ever after will forever disappoint them as a result. When, midway through the book, Anna discloses David's serial unfaithfulness, the narrator's response is telling: 'I was sorry she'd told me; I still wanted to believe that what they called a good marriage had remained possible, for some' (*Surf* 93). The narrator misses the obvious signs of their unhappiness, from the fact that Anna is not consulted about important plans, to David's sexist comments and Anna's sexually provocative behaviour as a result, to the fact that Anna is forced to strip as part of *Random Samples*. She sees one thing, when it is clear that another image is available.

Put simply, the novel acts as a palimpsestic text – a text that is layered over with meanings that erase and disrupt the picture that the reader receives. In art terms, a palimpsest is a parchment that has been partially erased and then painted or drawn over with another image. As the piece of art ages, the first image can bleed through, creating a new, hybrid image. Atwood's use of the palimpsest image is formally appropriate, given the fact that the main character and her lover are both artists. Where the narrator conveys a story of marriage and divorce, later revelations expose the truth, and rereadings of the text make this clear. At one point during their stay by the lake, Joe asks the narrator to marry him, but she refuses, saying she had done it before and did not want the pain: 'It was true, but the words were coming out of me like the mechanical words from a talking doll, the kind with the pull tape at the back; the whole speech was unwinding, everything in order, a spool' (*Surf* 81). This is indeed a rehearsed speech, though even she does not realize it at the time, so fully has she convinced herself of this version of her past. And yet, slightly odd and jarring images surface throughout her telling of this story. For example, in recalling her wedding, the narrator observes: 'I could recall the exact smells, glue and humid socks and the odour of second-day blouse and crystallized deodorant from the irritated secretary, and, from another doorway, the chill of antiseptic' (*Surf* 82). These seem like strange recollections, and it is significant that she focuses on smell and not on sight; she does not want to see the picture because it isn't real. She even recalls that her 'husband' treated her 'like an invalid rather than a bride' (*Surf* 82). The reason he doesn't treat her like a bride is because she isn't one: what this scene covers over is the fact that the narrator had a married lover who forced her to have an abortion in order to save his own marriage and family life, and what she is recalling is her acquiescence to his desire, an acquiescence for which she cannot forgive herself:

> It was all real enough, it was enough reality forever, I couldn't accept it, that mutilation, ruin I'd made, I needed a different version. I pieced it together the best way I could, flattening it, scrapbook, collate, pasting over the wrong parts. A faked album, the memories fraudulent as passports; but a paper house was better than none and I could almost live in it, I'd lived in it until now.   (*Surf* 137–8)

The narrator is only able to confront the reality that her fake past covered over once she accidentally comes across her father's body, submerged in the water where he was looking for rock paintings; his camera had kept him trapped and invisible. (The link between seeing and not seeing is crucial here.) Yet even at this point, upon discovering his body, she is not yet fully ready for reality, so she swims away, only for the body to be discovered by others, unrelated to her. Unable to cope with the explosion of her carefully constructed realities, she reverts to childhood behaviour that taught her to escape. Indeed, she reveals, 'The only defence was flight, invisibility' (*Surf* 129). First, though, she makes love to Joe – despite the fact that by this point they are partially estranged – because she is hoping to conceive a child. Yet this is a contradictory desire, as she also intends to leave the human world behind. It is perhaps not accidental that she is supposed to leave the island on the seventh day – the Christian symbolism having been sustained throughout the novel (though set alongside myth and legend, so that no world view is prioritized). The idea of constructing a new world is clearly apparent here. It is also significant that she chooses to make love to Joe outside the cabin, away from the confines of human habitation.

The narrator becomes, in Joan Larkin's words, 'unhuman' (Larkin in McCombs 50), and the reader must decide whether she is mad, whether she is a 'creative non-victim' or whether she is simply escaping again instead of confronting the reality of her situation. Her companions call her 'inhuman' (*Surf* 148) for her failure to communicate with them, but this is an inaccurate label; it is simply that she refuses to pretend to be civilized. She admits, 'From any rational point of view I am absurd; but there are no longer any rational points of view' (*Surf* 163). She dumps the exploitative film *Random Samples* into the lake and hides from her companions. What follows is a descent into the animal world, into possible madness and into a period where the narrator communes with the ghosts of her parents. In her animal state, she avoids certain areas as taboo, refuses to use human implements (in fact she destroys some) and sheds her clothing. She also becomes entirely filthy, refusing to groom herself (and by this point, she has no other animal or human to help her do so; indeed, grooming has been seen quite negatively in its association with Anna's false face). J. Brooks Bouson suggests that

> When the Surfacer … becomes transformed into the 'natural woman,' she both rebels against the masculinist mindset that maps and delimits the world and enacts her secret desire to escape from the contained, domestic sphere of femininity. But although she escapes masculine logic and domestic confinement in her merger with nature, and although the text insistently privileges nature over civilization, the Surfacer's transformation into the 'natural woman' is still unsettling.
>
> (Bouson 1993, 58)

Indeed, it becomes difficult to read her transformation, as Atwood relies on images rather than logic to move the narrative forward. Danielle Schaub suggests that rather than 'defining the self in relation to vast physical landscape', the novel defines 'landscape as internalised geographies of the self' (Schaub 85). This emphasis on the land connects with Northrop Frye's famous pronouncement that the central question of Canada is not 'Who am?' but 'Where is here?' (Frye 220).

Avoiding human food, the narrator induces a sort of trance-like state, and within this state, she finally sees her mother, feeding the birds, though 30 years younger than when she last saw her. A day later she encounters her father, in the shape of a wendigo or other mythical creature (perhaps a loup garou as in the fairy tales she is illustrating): 'It does not approve of me or disapprove of me, it tells me it has nothing to tell me, only the fact of itself' (*Surf* 181). This message is one she must consider overnight, its starkness hard to comprehend. The next morning, feeling she has somehow communed with her parents – 'I saw them and they spoke to me, in the other language' (*Surf* 182) – she finds herself reverting to her human nature, with all the loss that this entails. She understands that she will never encounter them again: 'from now on I'll have to live in the usual way, defining them by their absence; and love by its failures, power by its loss, its renunciation' (*Surf* 183). She then makes her famous claim about refusing to be a victim, about taking responsibility. At the end of the novel, Joe returns for her, and the narrator tenses towards him – but does not yet respond to the calling of her name. This ending, one of potential but not final movement, works well, in that it shows the lengths she has yet to travel in order to inhabit fully her humanity. Atwood's narrative endings – where resolutions are rarely offered, though images are stark and suggestive – work to unsettle the reader and keep the reader actively engaged in the story, long after the last page has been read.

Atwood's third novel, *Lady Oracle* (1976) again plays with identity. Atwood creates a comic female author who hides her popular costume Gothic romances from her Marxist husband, fearing his critical disdain. Within the novel, Atwood plays with critical responses and the confusion between creative output and 'real life' that seems to have dogged her own writing career. Moreover, she offers up a focus on celebrity, a recurring topic throughout her oeuvre. Atwood's protagonist starts life as Joan Delacourt, the overweight child of an unhappy mother, a girl who loves the spangle and sparkle of life and refuses to see that it sits uneasily on someone who does not embody the ideal of girlhood. Joan eventually transforms herself secretly into a successful Gothic novelist, so that she can inhabit her fantasies mentally and peddle them to others, from never-ending love to the idea that cruel men can, indeed, be heroes. She unexpectedly 'outs' herself as a writer when she produces a slim volume of poetry, *Lady Oracle*, under her married name, Joan Foster, and becomes a reluctant celebrity poet, complete with her own stalker (who may or may not be her artist lover). She is unready for celebrity and performs badly on talk shows. After a performance that she regrets, Joan bemoans, 'What was the use of being Princess-for-a-day if you still felt like a toad? Acted like one, too' (*LO* 238), and she is accosted by a fatuous artist who asks, '"Are you Lady Oracle?"' to which she replies, '"It's the name of my book"'. That Atwood has her character so enmeshed with her book that the audience inadvertently ties them into the same title (and that she then uses that title for her novel as a whole) offers just one example of the intricacies of celebrity and how it can be misunderstood. Eventually, Joan feels compelled to fake her own death as the only way to get out of the mess her life has become, and the novel opens once that she is on the metaphorical 'other side': 'The trick was to disappear without a trace, leaving behind me the shadow of a corpse, a shadow everyone would mistake for solid reality. At first I thought I'd managed it' (*LO* 7). Clearly, though, she hasn't, and the novel blends together Joan's present, hiding in a Mediterranean resort, with her past as a child and young adult, along with extracts of the Gothic novels she pens with such success.

As a character with more than one past, Joan seeks escape through interacting with characters who will not probe deeply or disturb her delicate balancing act. She not only thinks on her feet when confronted by dissonances between her self-created images, but she also does so while positioned in the circus imagery of balancing high on a tightrope. No doubt provoked by a diet of the Canadian National Exhibition escapades, Joan's circus personae include clowns, fat ladies, tightrope walkers and infamous escape artists. But these images, which she pulls on and off at whim, are overshadowed by her larger persona, that of Louisa K. Delacourt, writer of costume Gothics.

Joan is removed from politics, having despaired of ever catching up with her husband Arthur's current obsessions. Arthur consumes political goals much as Joan's readers do their costume Gothics: voraciously and repeatedly, searching out similar plots, only to be left ultimately unfulfilled. Joan literally and metaphorically shuts politics out of her writing by creating fictional pasts which take for granted a class structure, and by shutting the door between herself and her husband's political groups when doing so.

Critics interested in formulaic fiction point to the ideal nature of the fictional world. Readers, they believe, read such texts because the expected conclusions and stock elements of such tales relieve the burden of uncertainty so often associated with 'real life' (Cawelti 13). It is perhaps for this reason that Atwood's parody of the Gothic romance in *Lady Oracle* is so effective. Her

protagonist successfully follows conventional guidelines in her fictional novels while also patterning her own life against a Gothic narrative. As Joan's life
tumbles out of control, so her writing fails to conform to her familiar and comfortable guidelines, creating havoc and leading to unexpected conclusions.

Within Atwood's mock-Gothic larger work, she incorporates Louisa K.
Delacourt's various costume Gothics: *Stalked by Love*; *The Secret of Morgrave
Manor*; *The Lord of Chesney Chase*; *Escape from Love*; *Love, My Ransom*. The
last two have short excerpts included in the novel, while *Stalked by Love*, a
modern Gothic which pits the sensual Felicia (the current Lady Redmond)
against the virginal Charlotte, frames Joan's own story and includes several
separate passages. *Stalked by Love* is an appropriate subtitle for Joan's own
Gothic life; as Sybill Korff Vincent reveals, 'We are invited to compare [Joan's]
personal narrative with her works in progress, which represent a sub-text to
what she tells us about herself' (Vincent in Fleenor 158). Indeed, the various
incarnations of Lady Redmond in *Stalked by Love* take on the features of people
in Joan's life, and Redmond himself goes through many transformations. Significantly, the women in Joan's life are presented in her interpolated text as
separate, if similar, creatures in the centre of the maze at Redmond Grange,
whereas all the men are reduced to one being who has interchangeable faces.
Also significantly, there is no escape from the maze that Felicia (read Joan)
has knowingly entered. As one of the creatures in the maze reveals, there is
no going back (*LO* 342). There is only death, which Joan has already tried and
found wanting. However, the formula determines Felicia's eventual death; as
a deviant wife, she can neither hold Lord Redmond's love nor keep her place
at Redmond Grange – except at the centre of the mysterious maze. This leads
to difficulties for Joan, who has found herself acting out Felicia's role, rather
than the heroine's, which is her more normal role when 'automatically' writing
her books.

For *Escape from Love*, for example, Joan mimics the heroine Samantha
Deane's journey across Hyde Park – and ends up meeting her real-life 'hero'
instead – Arthur. For *Love, My Ransom*, Joan tells herself '*You are Penelope*'
(*LO* 219, author's italics) while experimenting with the supernatural, a topic
which her competitors have increasingly used to further their own sales. While
Joan eventually dismisses the supernatural from her costume Gothics (Penelope 'would have to make do with rape and murder like everyone else' (*LO*
223)), she uses her 'automatic writing' sessions as the basis for *Lady Oracle*, a
book of poetry which is repeatedly referred to in the text as 'a cross between
Kahlil Gibran and Rod McKuen' (*LO* 224).

In this way, Atwood presents two types of 'automatic writing' which are
both clearly shown to be anything but automatic. Though her sessions with

mirrors and candles reveal a few words not consciously written by Joan, her poems themselves are a product of her conscious thought: 'I would stare at these words, trying to make sense of them; I would look them up in *Roget's Thesaurus*, and most of the time, other words would fill in around them' (*LO* 221). This is similar to Joan's assertion that her other writing is also arrived at almost unconsciously: she writes them with her eyes closed (*LO* 131). However, by the very fact that Joan's costume Gothics conform to a set formula, one comes to realize that they are decidedly not automatic, but carefully structured. Indeed, Joan's need to 'act out' her scenes before she writes them also shows them to be constructed with forethought.

This desire to 'act out' the Gothic is not confined to Joan's enactments of her plots, however, but is clearly connected to Joan's compulsion to see the Gothic in her everyday life, however much she denies doing this. Atwood skilfully parodies the Gothic, then, not just in the texts which Joan pens, but also in the larger story of Joan's life. The ways in which Joan's life conforms to or resembles the Gothic relate directly or obscurely to the conventions of the Gothic as outlined by critics Joanna Russ and Eve Kosofsky Sedgwick. Russ somewhat flippantly categorises the Gothic thus:

> To a large, lonely, brooding *House* (always named) comes a *Heroine* who is young, orphaned, unloved, and lonely. She is shy and inexperienced. She is attractive, sometimes even beautiful, but she does not know it. Sometimes she has spent ten years nursing a dying mother; sometimes she has (or has had) a wicked stepmother, a bad aunt, a demanding and selfish mother (usually deceased by the time the story opens) or an ineffectual, absent, or (usually) long-dead father, whom she loves.
>
> (Russ 667–8)

Atwood parodies the single, brooding house which dominates the Gothic by providing a series of houses, most of them tacky and singularly lacking in mystery. Similarly, Atwood provides a character who does not appear to resemble the traditional heroine. Joan imagines herself as 'a Mediterranean splendor, golden-brown, striding with laughing teeth into an aqua sea, free at last' (*LO* 7), which neither tallies with the traditional picture of a beautiful but poor and frightened heroine, nor the reality of Joan's sunburnt, freckled skin and eyes 'the color and shape of cooked tomatoes' (*LO* 10). Yet, certain aspects of Joan *do* match Russ's categories. She is indeed lonely, though her separation from her family is of her own making, and she did feel unloved for a large portion of her young life. In addition, her red hair and slim body do make her attractive, while her previous incarnation as a fat woman prevents her from fully realizing this.

The character who most exactly fulfils Russ's stereotypes in Atwood's novel is the wicked mother, Fran Delacourt. Fran is no more than a spectral ghost during the 'present' sections of the novel at Terremoto. Yet she figures largely in Joan's remembered past, where she is represented as a monster (*LO* 67). Joan's father, too, resembles a Gothic father. 'Most of the time he was simply an absence' (*LO* 69), Joan recalls. Indeed, he figures minimally in the novel as a whole – absent from Joan's childhood, silent during her adolescence and remarried and moved away during her adulthood. Yet Atwood does provide him with several important Gothic scenes, all connected with death or resurrection. During the war, the reader is told (via Fran's drunken boasting) that Phil Delacourt acted as an assassin. During Joan's adolescence he is an anaesthetist who revives people who attempt suicide. Joan suspects him of murdering her mother (in a nice Gothic twist) but, like a traditional Gothic heroine, does not successfully investigate her suspicions. Joan reveals: 'I began to hunt for motives … But nothing turned up, and I abandoned my search a lot sooner than I would have if I'd been convinced. Besides, what would I have done if I'd found out my father was a murderer?' (*LO* 179).

Appropriately, it is Phil Delacourt's evidence which cuts short Joan's last escape, by convincing the press that Joan did not die by misadventure in her apparent drowning: he tells an interviewer that Joan had been a good swimmer, a fact which Joan is amazed that he knows (*LO* 314). This passage serves to reinforce the narrator's unreliability, since it questions the role that Joan's Gothic sensibilities have assigned to her father.

Russ also notes the presence of the Other Woman, the hero and his shadowy counterpart, the latter of whom are sometimes hard to distinguish (Russ 668, 669), and Atwood plays with each of these stock characters, too. The image of the Other Woman is undercut in Joan's retrospective narrative, since this role is assigned to Marlene, despite the fact that she is not engaged in a sexual contest with the heroine for the hero. However, enacting the role of the Gothic heroine demands that Joan find a female adversary. Thus, she compares herself unfavourably to Marlene, who is a mother, the managing editor of a magazine which Arthur joins, and an excellent cook – all of the things that Joan is not. Worse, she is, in fact, one of the Brownies who so tormented Joan as a child. Fittingly, Marlene is the woman who helps Joan to 'die'; the parody is effective. In a true Gothic novel the Other Woman would be plotting her death; in this novel she is merely a link in the plot that the heroine has hatched herself. Moreover, she is eventually arrested for Joan's 'murder' (*LO* 337).

In a Gothic novel, there are good men and bad men; the trick is to discover which is which. In *Lady Oracle*, Joan is taught that 'nice men did things for you, bad men did things to you' (*LO* 69), but Joan's early experiences lead her to realize that men can possibly be both. Consequently, in *Lady Oracle*, men evolve into one another, and boundaries are never fixed. This does not, however, keep Joan from seeking a Gothic hero to match her fantasies.

The first candidate for her Byronic figure is an 'Italian or Greek' short-order cook who calls himself John (*LO* 99). He is flirtatious, sprightly and determined to marry her, but, though Joan calls her association with him a sexual experience, John is hardly a Gothic hero, so she must set him aside. The parody is completed later in the novel when Joan comes across John again: he neither recognizes her nor remembers his former alias.

Joan's first lover, by contrast, does somewhat resemble a Gothic figure. He is titled (though calling him 'Paul the Polish Count' tends to deflect any serious appreciation of his status). He believes in gallantry, but his appearance undercuts his flair. Atwood makes him shorter than Joan with 'wispy light-brown hair receding from his forehead, sloping shoulders, and rimless spectacles, which were not fashionable at the time' (*LO* 145). Joan, accustomed to thinking in the Gothic mode, ignores these facets to concentrate on the parts of him which fit the Gothic hero. He is a significantly older, mysterious man with a past. He has survived unendurable conditions and escaped alive. Moreover, he owns a gun, has fits of jealousy and takes to following her.

Luckily, just as the Count begins to 'change', Joan meets Arthur. Deep in the Gothic mode, she misinterprets his impersonal advance and ends up cutting his cheek; his wound makes him highly desirable. She denies that she expects him to be a hero; she insists that she does not cloak him in fantasy, but her actions betray the truth. Arthur is stoic, unemotional and uninterested in Joan's past, but Joan either discounts these facets of his personality or turns them to advantage. Afraid to reveal her past to anyone, she remarks, 'Luckily he was never very curious about my past: he was too busy telling me about his' (*LO* 41). A true Gothic hero would not, of course, reveal himself so fully.

Accordingly, the list of possible heroes does not stop here. Atwood continually provides Joan with new objects for her affections, parodying both the Gothic structure of one man for one woman and the repetitive consumption of Gothic romances by their devoted readers. The fantasy is that one man is enough; the reality is that the reader needs a new fantasy man after finishing each novel. Thus, Joan next encounters the Royal Porcupine, whose connections to the Gothic include dressing up in capes, pretending that Joan is no one special at first and diving into moodiness (a trait Arthur shares). Finally, Joan falls for a reporter who comes to her hiding-place in Terremoto.

From this confusion of possible heroes, it is easy to deduce that there will also be a confusion of villains. In fact, the singular 'villain' of *Lady Oracle* is never explicitly determined, since several possibilities exist, including Arthur, the Royal Porcupine, Paul and the blackmailer Fraser Buchanan, who knows about Joan's secret writing. By following the Gothic pattern, however, Joan is unable to see that more than one man could be involved in the unsettling events which ultimately cause her to escape her Canadian life.

The final plot device that Russ examines in relation to the Gothic, the 'secret' (Russ 670), is multiply present in Atwood's text. Joan's past, present and future are all secrets, as are her mother's and father's pasts. In fact, Joan's future (her life after death, as it were) must remain a secret as a result of her secretive past and present activities. She is warned to '[a]void deception and falsehood; treat your lives as a diary you are writing and that you know your loved one will someday read, if not here on this side, then on the other side, where all the final reconciliations will take place' (*LO* 204). Typically, Joan does not heed this advice, which accounts for her need to fake her own death. Ironically, her life does become embodied in books, from her Gothic fantasies in her formula fiction, to her repressed emotions in her poetry, to her final biography/autobiography. Yet, this final confession of her past does not untangle all the secrets, for there are things she does not know, such as who really is attempting to frighten her and why her mother was so unhappy throughout her life. These facts remain ultimately undiscoverable.

Sedgwick's catalogue of Gothic conventions is more extensive than Russ's and focuses on images such as 'live burial' (Sedgwick 5), 'doubles', 'obscure family ties' and 'apparitions from the past' (Sedgwick 9). The most prominent example of live burial in Atwood's narrative is Joan's faked death in Lake Ontario.[2] This is not a forced confinement in the typical sense, but it is a necessary element for moving the plot forward. Yet other examples of live burial are also evident. Joan is buried in excess flesh throughout her childhood and adolescence, and the loss of her excess weight causes her to bury her past. She buries her clothes at the house in Terremoto and she later imagines these coming to life.

The most important Gothic doublings occur between Joan and her fictional constructs, or between Joan and her discarded personae: 'There was always that shadowy twin, thin when I was fat, fat when I was thin, myself in silvery negative ...' (*LO* 246). In addition, she believes that her public persona, her 'dark twin', wants to kill her and take her place, and that no one will stop this constructed double since 'the media were in on the plot, they were helping her' (*LO* 251). This is a particularly appropriate example, for not only does it show the culpability of the media, but it also exposes the 'crimes' that Joan as a Gothic writer performs herself: she creates characters who must die so that others might live happily. In her last novel, several wives die or disappear in order that another character might assume the title and the role of Lady Redmond. Thus, Felicia must die in order for Charlotte to take her place. Joan begins to realize what she is doing when she finds that her sympathy has switched sides. She asks, 'But what had [Felicia] ever done to deserve [death]? How could I sacrifice her for the sake of Charlotte? I was getting tired of Charlotte ...' (*LO* 319). The Gothic formula is failing her, both in her text and in her life.

However, Joan remains haunted by the spectral presence of her mother, although when she actively tries to resurrect her mother, she is unsuccessful. After Joan misses her mother's funeral, she attempts to conjure her up through the familiar ritual of gorging herself on the contents of the refrigerator: 'I kept expecting her to materialize in the doorway with that disgusted secretly pleased look I remembered so well – she liked to catch me in the act – but despite this ritual, which had often before produced her, she failed to appear' (*LO* 178). But this is no Gothic ritual, no true seance. When Joan attempts to contact the medium Leda Sprott, a figure from her adolescence, in the hopes of conjuring up her mother, she finds that the old woman has herself disappeared.

Yet the very Gothic experience of seeing her mother's ghost does occur three times. No apparitions other than her mother ever appear, and this is significant. Fran appears to Joan first when Joan is at a spiritualist meeting; at this point, Fran is still alive. Her second appearance occurs at the moment of her death and her third coincides with Joan's time on the 'other side' – after Joan has faked her own death. Each time Fran is wearing the same navy blue outfit and crying. The third time that she sees her mother's apparition, Joan seems to realize that this apparition is less a psychic event than a psychological one: 'She's never really let go of me because I had never let her go ... she had been my reflection for too long' (*LO* 329–30), she admits.

Fundamentally, as Coral Ann Howells argues, the novel is about 'storytelling, both the stories themselves and the writing process, for Joan offers us multiple narratives, figuring and refiguring herself through different fictional conventions' (Howells 2005, 55). It is therefore not accidental that at the end of this mock Gothic novel, Joan considers another future – that of a writer of science fiction – a genre Atwood would later take up herself with *The Handmaid's Tale*, *The Blind Assassin*, *Oryx and Crake* and *The Year of the Flood*.

Life Before Man (1979), though often given detailed examination in early critical texts on Atwood, has not had the sustained critical attention of her other work. What is key for this text is its focus on language (one passage details the many ideas associated with 'mummy') as well as emotional paralysis (a topic given more detailed – and arguably more successful – treatment in *The Handmaid's Tale*.) The novel follows the intertwined lives of Elizabeth and Nate Schoenhof, a married couple who live together but who no longer share a bed, and their various lovers, including Lesje Green and her lover William, as well as Nate's former lover Martha and Elizabeth's former lover

Chris. Central to the novel is the Royal Ontario Museum, where both Elizabeth and Lesje work, and metaphors of fossilization, stasis and decay abound. *Life Before Man* covers a period of almost two years, during which time the lovers revolve in and out of each others' lives, forming and reforming in different configurations: Nate and Lesje become lovers and eventually share a house, and Elizabeth seduces William in a bid to 'balance' the score, though almost half-heartedly. Martha haunts the edges, as a woman spurned by Nate, though oddly embraced by Elizabeth in a bid to keep her from gaining too much power, and Chris remains as a haunting presence. He is dead except in flashback and in one non-chronological entry, which slightly predates the rest of the story, but he haunts the text, and especially Elizabeth, who is unmade by his suicide but who refuses to allow herself to appear vulnerable.

Set between 1976 and 1978, the novel references the promise to hold a referendum on Quebec and other political and ecological issues; there is a marked male–female divide which seems to be set up, with Lesje, for example, afraid to admit that she does not care which side wins (acknowledging to herself that she would rather move than vote if she lived in Quebec, her lack of interest in politics stemming from a familial clash between cultures, prompting her to avoid outright choices between opposing sides), while William and to some extent Nate both pronounce their views outright. Elizabeth forthrightly claims: 'She's no more interested in elections than she is in football games. Contests between men, both of them, in which she's expected to be at best a cheerleader' (*LM* 51), clearly echoing the earlier Joan Foster in her views of men's games. Yet Atwood also works to deconstruct such gender divides, particularly through Nate's mother, a political activist who continues to cajole Nate into having a social conscience.

Given this political backdrop, readers might expect the novel to deal more overtly with feminism as a political movement, but, in fact, neither principal female character is touched positively by feminism: Lesje is afraid she has not suffered enough at the hands of men and finds gatherings of women frightening: 'Even in the women's group she went to in graduate school, mostly because her roommate shamed her into it, she'd been cautious, afraid of saying the wrong thing; of being accused' (*LM* 54). Lesje even claims, 'It would be no good to say that she was just a scientist, she wasn't political. According to them, everything was political' (*LM* 55). This 'them' is directed at other women; in the present tense of the novel, her interactions with other women focus on lunch and shopping, though she is comfortable with neither venture, as this play on words indicates: 'She flips through the racks, looking for something that might become her, something she might become' (*LM* 18). She does indeed seem to be an unfinished character, one who absorbs what others claim about her. About her first lover, she acknowledges, 'she's no longer waiting for William to propose to her' (*LM* 21), though she does appear to be waiting for something. Marriage was the goal she thought she was following, but she discovers that William 'finds her impossibly exotic. True, he loves her, in a way. He bites her on the neck when they make love' (*LM* 21). This casual entwining of love and potential violence returns later in the novel, but, for now, this could be read merely as a voracious kind of love, though that does not chime with William the Wasp, as she calls him, and his apparently reserved nature. Later, when the relationship breaks down, she finds it hard to know how to feel. Not only does she not have the words for the assault she suffers at William's hands, but she cannot frame their relationship into a version that makes sense. If marriage and divorce are things that 'create a framework, a beginning, and ending' (*LM* 184), she cannot successfully interpret the ending of her relationship with William, and she cannot comprehend that his sexual violence is part of a larger social problem.

Angry with her (perhaps at the discovery of her affair with Nate, though this is not made explicit), William attempts to rape Lesje, and succeeds in sexually violating her. She manages, it seems, to avoid him penetrating her, but even this is not entirely clear: 'She clamps her legs together, tightens the muscles of her neck and shoulders, and lets William batter himself against her. He's pulling her hair now, digging his fingers into her arms. Finally he groans, oozes, unclenches' (*LM* 178). Lesje's response to this assault is confused: 'Lesje is afraid he's going to cry. Then she will have to forgive him … It's the sight of William turning into someone else that has shocked her. She doesn't know whose fault it is' (*LM* 178). Implicitly, she seems to be accepting some aspect of fault herself, reinforcing the flawed assumption of female culpability in male violence. Her lack of language to do with assault is clear in the following passage:

> The day after that thing happened – she doesn't know what to call it and has finally decided to think of it as *the incident* – William left early in the morning … She resisted the desire to phone Nate and describe *the incident*. After all it wasn't that bad, she hadn't been hurt, she hadn't really been raped, not technically.   (*LM* 185)

She chooses silence in the face of sexual violation, and is unable to see that a supporting feminist framework would help her interpret 'the incident' as what it is. Elizabeth, in contrast, might seem initially to be more of a feminist icon, claiming at one point, 'She doesn't glance into the store windows; she knows what she looks like and she doesn't indulge in fantasies of looking any other way. She doesn't need her own reflection or the reflection of other people's ideas of her or of themselves' (*LM* 49). Elizabeth has an important job, combines it successfully with motherhood, and is clearly a fighter and the family breadwinner. She is also in charge, it seems, of her own sexuality, choosing to have relationships outside of her marriage. Yet this ability to fight against societal norms is later revealed as fundamentally damaged, her sexuality and apparent sexual liberation actually masking a far more worrying response: rebellion against authority rather than an indication of pleasure. Sex for Elizabeth is about power and control alone, and she believes – falsely it turns out – that she is able to control men through this power.

The novel opens just after Chris's suicide, at a point where no one quite knows how to behave, including Elizabeth, who veers between anger and apathy. Elizabeth is introduced to the reader as a first-person narrator, claiming, 'I don't know how I should live. I don't know how anyone should live. All I know is how I do live. I live like a peeled snail' (*LM* 3). This image, Lorna Irvine argues, 'suggests disintegration and a puzzling kind of exposure' (Irvine 267) and it seems as if the reader might be in for a difficult mental journey towards recovery, told from Elizabeth's fragile perspective. However, the expectations set up by this opening are dismantled as the novel progresses, because the first-person narration is only intermittent. Most of the novel follows the three protagonists in third person, consecutively going through the same days at first, though later this rigid pattern is disturbed. Each of the first three sections begins with Elizabeth, with Lesje and Nate taking turns in the middle position of the triangle; the fourth section begins with Lesje and the fifth with Nate, and only here is it apparent that Elizabeth is now in the middle of the relationship between Lesje and Nate rather than the other way around.

That Atwood sets up this pattern and expectation is intriguing – the characters move from within rigid, necessary patterns to chaos as the novel progresses. Frank Davey goes so far as to argue that 'the chapters appear as independent, discrete units which juxtapose in a nearly static structure rather than merge into a developing shape' (Davey 1984, 82).

Of the three, it is clear that most of the characters, including Lesje, believe Elizabeth to be the most interesting character in the novel; Lesje even recalls thinking that in the previous love triangle, between Elizabeth, Chris and Nate, Nate was 'simply the least interesting figure' (*LM* 56). It is certainly the case that Elizabeth harbours secrets revealed to the reader but to few of her companions. She is referred to as 'haute Wasp' (*LM* 88) by Lesje's friends, and though she was raised by a wealthy aunt, Auntie Muriel, she was the child of an alcoholic and homeless mother and an unreliable father. This is a secret past she does not reveal, though one she relies on to mount attacks that her adversaries do not see coming:

> They don't know she's a refugee, with a refugee's desperate habits. Nate knows a little of it. Chris knew it, finally. Martha doesn't, and neither does Lesje, and this gives Elizabeth a large advantage. She knows there's

> nothing in her that will compel her to behave decently. She can speak from that other life if she has to. If pushed she'll stop at nothing. Or, put another way: when she reaches nothing she will stop.   (*LM* 142)

Indeed, even in a dinner-party game, where individuals must convince the others not to throw them overboard should there be a shipwreck and limited space on a life raft, Elizabeth reveals ' "I have a very strong survival instinct. If you try to push me overboard, I'll take at least one of you down with me" ' (*LM* 148).

Most of Elizabeth's power comes through language, her ability to speak in different registers, the 'genteel chic she's acquired, which is a veneer but a useful one' (*LM* 140) and the language of the streets; she uses language as a tool against Lesje and Nate, and against her Auntie Muriel as an adult. She refuses to be seen as a victim, and it is perhaps this steely resolve that is the saddest element of her character. She 'refuses to be deserted against her will' (*LM* 196), so she claims to be in charge of their separation. She fights to retain her dignity but with the loss of all personal feelings. At one point she claims: 'She isn't trying to torture Nate: torture is a by-product. She's merely trying to win. Looking at him, watching him subside back onto his chair, she knows she will win, there's no way she can help winning. She'll win, and she hopes it will make her feel better' (*LM* 255). Yet this hoped-for resolution seems unlikely, as she holds onto her anger and hurt and betrayal, despite being guilty of inflicting each of these things onto Nate previously.

If Elizabeth is a fully formed if flawed character, Lesje, as we have seen, is less fully formed. She accidentally becomes involved with Nate, because she found it hard to refuse his invitation to lunch, and she remains involved with him because he presents himself as a gift to her. But this gift comes with strings attached, including becoming the person he thinks she is:

> The fact is that she's addicted to Nate's version of her … He expects her to be serene, a refuge; he expects her to be kind. He really thinks she is, underneath, and that if he can dig into her far enough this is what he'll unearth. He ought to be able to tell by now that she isn't like this at all. Nevertheless she wants to be; she wants to be this beautiful phantom, this boneless wraith he's conjured up. Sometimes she really does want it.
>
> (*LM* 259)

Nate has in fact, constructed her, and thinks she is 'without rules' as opposed to his rule-bound wife (*LM* 155). Lesje remains indistinct to him throughout the novel, in stark relief to his close-up view of Elizabeth. His lover 'glimmers like a thin white moon for him alone' (*LM* 238), he thinks, though he's afraid she'll find out he isn't made of any substance himself. Perhaps this is a rational fear, because Nate does seem, like Lesje, to be unable to move forward or to take responsibility for his future. He waits for Elizabeth to kick him out, despite realizing even before Chris's death that 'at some vague place in the future he himself will need to leave her' (*LM* 228). His leaving is, however, incremental and passive.

Coral Ann Howells argues that Nate continually reinvents himself and therefore 'occupies multiple identities' (Howells 2005, 71), but I would argue that he simply cannot place himself – and perhaps does not want to be placed: hence his failure as a business man and maker of children's toys, as well as his failure as a lawyer and a husband. Moreover, he seems incapable of seeing beyond his own particular perspective. His view of all women is suspect, including his former lover Martha, whom he believes to be more refined than she is, and less capable. When he hears that she wants to retrain as a lawyer, moving beyond her current duties as legal secretary, he only partially re-evaluates her as possibly good enough 'for family court' (*LM* 267). In relation to his activist mother, he retains an optimistic belief that she is 'always willing to take the children, always waiting in fact for chances just like these. After all, she's their grandmother' (*LM* 276). He simply cannot imagine any other scenario; she is there to serve him, at a moment's notice. Therefore, when she casually relates the fact that she took up activism to stave off her own despair after the death of her husband and to find a reason to live, he is horrified. He cannot accept that she had considered suicide despite his existence, and must therefore reject that world-altering view. It is telling that just after this revelation, he physically breaks free from both mother and daughters, and realizes that his greatest fantasy is to find 'that nonexistent spot where he longs to be. Mid-air' (*LM* 280).

The novel ends in mid-air, it seems. Nate is on a run, unaware that Lesje's plotted pregnancy has come to fruition. Lesje is preparing for single parenthood, and significantly it is only in her own final section that Lesje displaces both Elizabeth and Nate from the centre of her universe; the imagined baby takes that space instead. It remains telling that Lesje herself never occupies it. Finally, Elizabeth is surveying her latest exhibit at the museum. The opening and closing sections belong to Elizabeth and structurally this is important – she is the key to it all, the main force around whom the others whirl.

Atwood's fifth novel, *Bodily Harm* (1981), follows a 'lifestyle tourist', Rennie Wilford, who uses faux-fads as a substitute for involvement with others. She eventually learns that she must not only seek, but also initiate, involvement. Indeed, the term 'massive involvement', used initially in the novel to describe her breast cancer, becomes a metaphor for her own place in the world, and in this way, the novel follows Atwood's own growing politicization and involvement in organizations such as Amnesty International. The novel picks up on some (by now) familiar Atwood tropes: wordplay (both 'massive involvement' and 'terminal' take on multiple meanings in the book); fragmentation, especially of the body; mirrors and surfaces; and a Gothic romance narrative that in many respects fails to conform to its expected outcome, with rescue a goal but not a firm reality.

It is the body which is most fragmented, from the missing sections of Rennie's cancerous breast to the image of mannequins strapped into pornographic poses by an artist Rennie tries to interview, to the recurring image of hands, cut off from the body, that haunt the text. Rennie avoids mirrors once she is (in her view) damaged, but they are peppered throughout the novel, even as she turns away from them. Her insistent focus on the present is both one of belligerence and of fear – after her diagnosis, and remission, she fears the future and does not fully believe in its existence. Instead, she continues to play with surfaces, deliberately trying to keep things light and at a distance (though her insistent touching of the surface of her breast belies her initial focus on surfaces and reveals her almost unconscious fear of depths). Although others claim that she can see the future, given that her predictions of trends sometimes come to fruition (and in fact she even makes up trends to see if she has the power to make them occur), Rennie argues instead, 'I see into the present, that's all. Surfaces. There's not a whole lot to it' (*BH* 26). She insists that surfaces are 'preferable to depths' (*BH* 211) and goes out of her way to avoid any deep thinking or reflection on her life, her world view, or her future.

Rennie is deliberately off-centre, and seeks the sidelines rather than the limelight, taking in the message of her mother's world in the small town of Griswold, where decency is more important than love and where the worst thing one can do is stand out or make a fuss. As she reveals, 'As a child I learned three things well: how to be quiet, what not to say, and how to look at things without touching them' (*BH* 54). As an adult, she has learned these lessons so well that she cannot get past them and once she finds herself in a seriously dangerous situation – on an island rocked by political assassinations, money and drugs-running – she finds herself thinking of herself as part of a tacky movie or a bad novel instead of confronting reality. As a distancing technique, it works – until in the final section of the novel when she is trapped in jail with her acquaintance Lora, a woman with whom Rennie has only accidentally become entangled and whom she does not even like.

As with many an Atwoodian character, Rennie is a flawed heroine, and her final fate is tantalizingly unclear. Is she rescued from her prison cell in a Caribbean island, or not? The reader may, optimistically, read the ending as what-actually-happens; but the insistent use of the future tense in the last section of the novel suggests that this possible future remains only a possibility,

and Rennie herself may well be unrescuable. But from what is she to be rescued? A Caribbean jail? Her own bodily 'massive involvement'? Or her deter-
mination to live a life of surfaces? The answer may be all three. What is clear
is that Atwood sets up a narrative that seeks to question narrative in the first
place, particularly in its use of a Gothic framework and stories.

Coral Ann Howells calls the novel 'a peculiarly fragmented text' (Howells
2005, 83) and it is certainly true that it moves between times, places and tenses
(using past, present and future tenses) almost randomly, as if it is a series of
stories rather than a singular, coherent narrative. Indeed, so fragmented is the
text that critics have argued over its 'real' setting, with Lorna Irvine suggesting that the Caribbean cell is really a cover for a hospital ward where Rennie
may – or may not – be recovering from cancer. Irvine helpfully points out the
similarity between the imagery of the jail cell and that of the hospital room/
bed (Irvine in Van Spanckeren and Castro 93), though most critics take the jail
cell as read, and as an important reminder of how politics invades the here and
now. As Rennie says, in the midst of her most traumatic experience, 'there's
no longer a *here* and a *there*. Rennie understands for the first time that this is
not necessarily a place she will get out of, ever. She is not exempt. Nobody is
exempt from anything' (*BH* 290, italics in original). At the same time, Irvine's
suggestion of an alternative reading of Rennie's stories should make the careful reader pause. After all, there are moments in the text that stand out as
unreadable. Near the end of the novel, for example, this passage occurs: 'Pretend you're really here, she thinks. Now: what would you do?' (*BH* 284). This
is a lone passage, two short sentences together, and there's no context for
this discussion: what pretence is she undertaking – that she's in jail, or elsewhere? Elaine Tuttle Hansen calls passages like these 'unruly' because their
'exact relationship to the underlying storyline or plausible sequence of events
remains permanently unclear' (Hansen 7). Atwood does not make it easy for
the reader – or her heroine – to work out exactly what is going on, and it's no
coincidence that when Rennie is idly reading murder mysteries on her holiday,
she 'doesn't have much patience for the intricacies of clues and deductions'
(*BH* 246). Instead, she charges through descriptions of women's mutilated
bodies, which are described almost lovingly by the detectives sent to uncover
the truth; she does not expect to deal with such realities herself.

The use of multiple stories (and storytellers, for Lora also takes up first-person
narration at times) offers Atwood a chance to explore who tells what stories
when, and to what effect, from stories of individual heroism or danger, to stories of national identity and crisis. No perspective is really privileged; all are
shown to be in some way contingent. As Rennie's temporary lover Paul suggests
of the island, '"In this place you get at least three versions of everything, and

if you're lucky one of them is true. That's if you're lucky"' (*BH* 150). Rennie is cancer survivor, travel writer, political prisoner; Paul is political and agricultural adviser, potential CIA informant or agent, drug runner or potential rescuer. Lora is an abuse survivor, a woman skating on the edge of legality (and sometimes tipping over it) or simply 'one of those women you meet in bars in foreign countries, who seem not to have chosen anything but merely ended up wherever they happen to be, and it's too much effort for them to go home' (*BH* 91). Lora's boyfriend Prince is a political dupe, a political player or a naive boy playing at politics, and his opponents Ellis and Dr Minnow are read multiply in the text, as heroes or villains themselves. There is no *one* reading of anyone, partly because, as Paul reveals, Rennie is suffering from ' "Alien reaction paranoia" ' or the inability to distinguish between what is dangerous and what is not (*BH* 76), and partly because ' "[t]here's no good guys and bad guys, nothing you can count on, none of it's permanent any more, there's a lot of improvisation" ' (*BH* 240). Building on her critical work on victimization, Atwood outlines the fact that ' "There's only people with power and people without power. Sometimes they change places, that's all" ' (*BH* 240).

Broken into six long sections, with gaps in between passages (signified sometimes, though not always, by a large black circular symbol), the novel moves back and forth between past and present, between Toronto and St Antoine and Ste Agathe, two Caribbean islands which Rennie visits in order to write an anodyne travel piece. As Rennie notes, 'Ordinarily she would have done some homework, but she was in too much of a hurry. This time she's flying blind' (*BH* 17). She is flying so blind that she does not realize she has arrived just as the islands have their first elections after the British colonial rulers have left. Thus, despite her intentions, Rennie accidentally becomes involved in the politics of the place and even seems to have been used as a pawn in an illegal trade in guns and drugs.

Rennie has gone to St Antoine to get away from it all – 'all' being her breakup with her live-in lover Jake, following her mastectomy, and her ill-fated infatuation with her surgeon Daniel, who, she feels, rescued her. (The need for rescue is a recurring motif in the novel.) Moreover, Rennie has recently been the victim of a senseless crime – or the potential victim of a serious one: she returns home to her apartment to find policemen inspecting her house and a coiled rope on her bed, signifying violence and sexual trauma. As Howells argues, this opening image offers up 'a perfect connection between her fears of death from cancer and external physical violence, just as it also signals the perversion of sexual desire when the male erotic gaze becomes the hostile scrutiny of a rapist or a killer' (Howells 2005, 84). The policemen here act not as defenders of the innocent but as arbiters of guilt: after all, the policeman 'wanted it to be my fault, just a little, some indiscretion, some provocation. Next he would start lecturing me about locks, about living alone, about safety' (*BH* 15). Rennie as victim is assumed to be Rennie as accomplice, with her behaviour, rather than her intruder's, under scrutiny and found wanting. It is therefore significant that once Rennie goes to the Caribbean island, she *does* become an unwitting accomplice (and she has previously been complicit in her lover Jake's sadistic sexual fantasies). Rennie goes to the Caribbean to take photographs, but not to see; to be neutral and invisible, uninvolved, but the insistent focus on seeing and not seeing betrays her assumed innocence as tourist. Rennie thinks that this role means she can 'keep her options open' (*BH* 227) and be exempt from pain. She soon learns, however, that although she thinks that she and other tourists can 'look all they want to, they're under no obligation to see' (*BH* 185), it is the very act of seeing that will rescue her (if anything does).

Rennie is used to telling stories; she does it for a living, and she does it to entertain her fellow acquaintances. Yet there are stories she cannot tell. For example, she tells no one about her intruder, for fear it will make her sound like a man-hater. Like many Atwoodian heroines, she has a fear of organized feminism, and dismisses feminists as wanting stories of pain and trauma, of not being able to get past outdated notions such as sexual harassment; she even delights, initially, when Jake tells her that he likes her for her body, not her mind. Rennie's world view cannot accept the reality of sexual violence, and so she tries to deny – even to herself – her fear of Jake's sexual aggression: 'A secure woman is not threatened by her partner's fantasies, Rennie told herself. As long as there is trust' (*BH* 106). The insistent 'Rennie told herself' belies the truth – that she is threatened by Jake's sex-play rape fantasies. Similarly, when she is commissioned to write a light 'lifestyle' piece on pornography, unlike the 'heavy and humourless' treatment given the topic by radical women's magazines that 'missed the element of playfulness' (*BH* 207), Rennie initially plays along. Keith is sufficiently aware to know that he has to get a woman to write the piece, but it turns out that Rennie cannot package this as entertainment. What she sees at the public police exhibition make her physically ill, a reaction that makes it impossible for her to carry on with the sex games that Jake likes to play.

These are stories Rennie cannot tell, despite her proficiency with language. Indeed, in the jail cell with Lora, she finds herself outdone by her companion's stories of actual physical and sexual abuse: 'Rennie knows what she's supposed to feel: first horror, then sympathy. But she can't manage it. Instead she's dejected by her own failure to entertain. Lora has better stories' (*BH* 271). These 'better stories' put Lora into the position of victim, a role Rennie assigns to her to avoid assigning it to herself. But she isn't a good reader of the stories;

she misreads Lora's nature and her resolve. In prison, she is disgusted with Lora for trading her body for chewing gum (having deliberately kept herself in ignorance about what transactions occur out of her eye line), but in fact, Lora is trading her body in the hope of being reunited with Prince, and it is only when she finds out that he is actually dead that Lora loses her capacity to deal with their degradation and lashes out at their captors.

Roberta Rubenstein argues that Lora is 'Rennie's own darker double, the other face of her own being, the woman whose exposure to violent sexual abuse from childhood makes her the symbolic female scapegoat for patriarchal exploitation' (Rubenstein 273). Hence, the image of Lora as endlessly violated – perhaps in contrast to Rennie. Lora thinks less of Rennie because she is too precious to put out; and indeed, in the one instance where it appears that Rennie will be the subject of sexual abuse in the prison, she is 'saved' by Lora's violent reaction to Prince's death. Finally, Lora becomes the ultimate victim of any mystery: the violated blonde who both 'asks for it' and definitely receives it – perhaps as far as death.

It is in confronting Lora's abused and broken body, rather than turning away from it as she wants to, that Rennie reconnects with morality. Having pleaded with others, silently, for rescue, having assumed that Paul or others will indeed become the Gothic heroes she so desires, Rennie understands that only she has the power, after all. Taking Lora's hands into her own, she wills the other woman to live: 'Surely, if she can only try hard enough, something will move and live again, something will get born' (*BH* 299). It is no accident that the recurring image of hands – hands that heal, hands that are missing, hands that are shaken or held, hands that are kept in check, hands that are dirty – litter the text. Thus, in being confronted with Lora's possibly lifeless body, Rennie becomes the novel's hero herself, reaching out and embracing the hands she had previously not wanted to touch. A long passage that reveals Rennie's inner struggle is made up of run-on sentences, outlining Rennie's struggle, and finishing with the lines, 'she can't do it, it will have to do, it's the face of Lora after all, there's no such thing as a faceless stranger, every face is someone's, it has a name' (*BH* 299). She hears – or imagines that she hears – Lora's voice: 'Was that real? She's afraid to put her head down, to the heart, she's afraid she will not be able to hear' (*BH* 299).

Whether Lora lives, or Rennie escapes, is never finally known; the novel ends with a future-tense imagining of a return to Canada, and of being asked by Canadian officials not to tell this story, since it would disrupt the allocation of aid for peaceful development. Yet the lasting image of Lora's hands offers the hope that she will tell, finally, if she ever is released, as Lora had begged her to: 'She can feel the shape of a hand in hers, both of hers, there but not there,

like the afterglow of a match that has gone out. It will always be there now'
(*BH* 300).

Howells believes that *Bodily Harm* reveals that 'disengagement and escape
may be possible only in fantasy' (Howells in Kroetsch and Nischik 131); the
more important story is one of connection, action and resistance. It thus sets
up the reader well for Atwood's most famous novel to date, *The Handmaid's
Tale*, which offers a horrifying dystopia that again reveals the fundamental
need for women's stories to be heard.

The Handmaid's Tale (1985) remains Atwood's most frequently taught text
and is often the student's first introduction to her work. Five years after it was
published, it was made into an unsuccessful film. The adaptation did not work
because Hollywood's requirement for a feisty and successful heroine was at
odds with Offred's necessary passivity. However, in 2000 it was adapted into
a successful opera that has seen a number of international performances. It is
the only one of Atwood's novels to expand beyond its original format in this
way and this is testament to its enduring legacy. The novel's power resides in
its clear depiction of a future dystopia, a vision that recalls earlier dystopias
such as Aldous Huxley's *Brave New World*, George Orwell's *1984* and Evgeny
Zamyatin's *We*. Alternatively defined as science fiction, dystopic nightmare,
futuristic prophecy, slave narrative or satiric romance,[3] *The Handmaid's Tale*
expands beyond such limiting frameworks as it explores a potential future. Jill
LeBihan connects the tale with the protagonist herself, a woman known only
by the patronymic Offred: 'like the unconventional narrator of the tale, the
Handmaid herself, who keeps at least one of her identities secret, *The Handmaid's Tale* similarly resists labels that position it within a particular generic
stream' (LeBihan in Howells and Hunter 96). Like most of Atwood's work,
then, the novel offers a number of routes into exploring its plot, structure and
perspective.

Atwood clearly situates most of the novel in a near future, one where our
everyday experiences get transformed into something sinister. The reader's
guide to this world, Offred, is amongst the first wave of handmaids (women
who are forced to bear children for infertile, privileged couples), and she offers
us the perspective of a recent captive, one who must adjust to the new totalitarian regime of Gilead. Contemporary society's easy reliance on and unthinking
acceptance of computer data storage of personal information, genetic modifi-
cation and a myriad of other scientific interventions (including fertility treatment), or the world's complacency in the face of environmental shifts are all
under scrutiny in the novel as they lead to this new society, where women are
placed in strict gender roles (signified by their clothing) and men of power
keep everyone in check. In addition to these overt mechanisms for control,

fear of betrayal and inculcated self-surveillance keep others from speaking out: there is no one an individual can trust.

In Gilead, 'Freedom from' is elevated above 'Freedom to' and this re-visioning of authority as liberty is just one example of how language is purposely corrupted. With reading restricted, and visual signs replacing written ones in order to transform a literate public into an illiterate one, history is reconstructed in the novel. New words enter the vocabulary, some such as Compuphone, Computalk and Compubank, representing technology. Others represent the new reality of a fearful theocracy: Salvagings, Prayvaganzas and Particicution. Prayvaganzas, for example, are large gatherings of people for particular rituals: 'Women's Prayvaganzas are for group weddings … usually. The men's are for military victories. These are the things we are supposed to rejoice in the most, respectively' (*HT* 232). Particicution is the participatory execution of apparent criminals, a way of reinforcing the behaviour of a crowd of handmaids and also a vent for their frustration and enforced passivity.

The women of Gilead are strictly segregated into handmaids, fertile women who bear children for Commanders; Commanders' Wives, whose redundancy and enforced domesticity have no real outlets; Marthas, who undertake domestic work; Econowives, working-class women who have to undertake a number of functions, and Aunts, women of nominal power who enforce the regulations. Only the Aunts have access to the written word, and in return for this power, they re-educate the women into their roles. The men, too, are segregated, into Guardians, Angels, Eyes and Commanders, and everyone watches everyone else for slips and transgressions. As Offred's Commander notes, '"Better never means better for everyone … It always means worse, for some"' (*HT* 222). Under this new regime, scripture is altered to fit the regime's purpose, and familiar sayings become new scripture, often with their original meanings destroyed or removed: 'Pen Is Envy, Aunt Lydia would say, quoting another Centre motto, warning us away from such objects' (*HT* 196). The move from Freudian 'penis envy' to its literal manifestation – the pen as penis, the pen and penis both equating with power – reveals not only Atwood's clever wordplay but also how the tools and knowledge of individuals can be used against them.

Like *Surfacing*, *The Handmaid's Tale* is a palimpsestic text, so much so that Atwood uses the term itself early in the novel, when she describes the gym that imprisons the new handmaids. Looking around the room that used to be the setting for sports and high-school dances, Offred muses, 'the music lingered, a *palimpsest* of unheard sounds, style upon style, an undercurrent of drums, a forlorn wail, garlands made of tissue paper flowers, cardboard devils, a revolving ball of mirrors, powdering the dancers with a snow of light' (*HT* 13, italics mine). Reference to the ritual of sexual exploration is not accidental, for though the handmaids are required to submit to sexual intercourse with their Commanders monthly in the hopes of achieving a pregnancy, sexual passion is entirely set aside and love no longer exists, at least not officially. Sex is a function, and a symbolic one in this novel, with the Commander's Wife symbolically sharing the bed on which the conception is hoped to take place, so that she can move into the role of mother once the child is born (though only if it is normal; if it is not, it is discarded as an 'unbaby' or a 'shredder', to use the handmaids' colloquial phrase).

The novel overlays past and present, which bump up against each other, and the narrative moves between sections entitled Night, where Offred appears most real and most alone, and those sections that are (implicitly) Day sections, which have other names and other functions. Offred, known to be fertile because she'd borne a daughter, becomes a handmaid when her marriage is annulled by the state. She is touched in ceremony, but not in love, and there is a lingering sense of shame and guilt around the handmaid's role.

She had hoped that the Wife of her new Commander would become friends with her, 'an older sister, a motherly figure, someone who would understand and protect' her (*HT* 26). She yearns to speak over coffee to the Marthas of the household, Cora and Rita, and she notes that it is 'as if the voice itself were a traveller, arriving from a distant place. Which it would be, which it is' (*HT* 21). But coffee and conversation are forbidden to the handmaids, and her role makes her despised by the other women in the house. Even when one of the Commander's Marthas unexpectedly offers a small kindness, Offred is so inculcated into her role that she tells us, 'I would rather have the disapproval, I feel more worthy of it' (*HT* 145).

Conversely, Offred says of her partner Ofglen, before they became confidantes, 'Sometimes I wish she would just shut up and let me walk in peace' (*HT* 29). The conversation in which she would engage with the Marthas, talking about aches and pains and the weather, is like the old conversations she might have had and taken for granted, or even been irritated with. The ritualized conversations she is allowed to have with Ofglen, however, only reinforce the reality of the present Gilead.

The past is spoken of with more than a little nostalgia (not least because of the presence of her daughter and husband), and this is true even of the negative aspects of her apparently free society; in contrast, the narrator's voice becomes distinctly more impersonal when relating 'present' events. As Offred notes, 'One detaches oneself. One describes' (*HT* 106). The 'present' events are the daily facts of Offred's slavery. Offred leads the reader through her days and nights, coolly explaining what function she serves and how she serves it:

> My red skirt is hitched up to my waist, though no higher. Below it the Commander is fucking. What he is fucking is the lower part of my

> body. I do not say making love, because this is not what he is doing. Copulating too would be inaccurate, because it would imply two people and only one is involved.   (*HT* 104)

Offred denies that the Ceremony is a form of rape, admitting, 'nothing is going on here that I haven't signed up for. There wasn't a lot of choice but there was some, and this is what I chose' (*HT* 105). However, choice is a problematic issue in Gilead. Although one of the Aunts argues that the society that predates Gilead, the modern USA, was '"a society dying … of too much choice"' (*HT* 35), the problem was not choice but apathy, not too much freedom but too little activity in the face of growing political and environmental threats. Offred acknowledges this: 'We lived, as usual, by ignoring. Ignoring isn't the same as ignorance, you have to work at it' (*HT* 66). Indeed, it is for this very reason that Atwood chooses Offred as her voice of Gilead: because she is *not* heroic. She is, instead, a passive everywoman, awaiting rescue, and maintaining, even in the midst of the regime, some comfort in ignorance.

Offred's very name indicates her role. Offred is literally 'Of Fred'. Her connection to her Commander is one of belonging (to, not with); the echo of former rituals is not accidental. After all, many women still change their surnames upon marriage, indicating another kind of possession. Critics have argued that Offred's name symbolizes her position in other ways, too: she is off-red, or not quite fully aligned with her role; she is offered up; she is off-read, as in mis-read, and she is afraid (Kaler 47). Moreover, the lack of a confirmed original name indicates another stripping of her identity (though canny critics have surmised that her name was originally June, as it is in the list of names offered at the very beginning of the novel, and the only one not assigned to another handmaid).

The jumbled glimpses the reader gets of Offred's life before Gilead serve both as reasons for her to try to remain prepared for escape and as channels of fantasy to keep reality from intruding too much. Atwood has always used punctuation in her own unique way, and in this novel, her style reflects the loose connection between fantasy and reality. For example, Atwood connects diverse things with mere commas, which serve to show the reader how easy it is to slip into the fantasy mode or role: 'We wait, the clock in the hall ticks, Serena lights another cigarette, I get into the car. It's a Saturday morning, it's a September, we still have a car' (*HT* 94). Offred spends much of her time waiting, and it's no coincidence that this passage concerns preparation for the Ceremony, or Offred's mental flight from it into a past with her husband Luke. Offred is deprived of most of the other escapes allowed in Gilead: alcohol, which is available to the Wives; men's clubs, where the Commanders gather and engage in illicit activities such as gambling and prostitution. Offred is allowed only one small respite – a relationship, of sorts, with Nick, the Commander's chauffeur.

Yet even this relationship is compromised, set up as it is by the Commander's Wife, for the purpose of impregnating Offred, and it remains unclear whether this is a respite also for Nick, or just another assignment.

It is in the Commander's study that the reader becomes most aware of Offred's deprivations, not materially, but physically and psychologically. Offred is summoned to the Commander's study one evening for an illicit game of Scrabble, and further meetings follow. Offred notes: 'I know I need to take it seriously, this desire of his. It could be important, it could be a passport, it could be my downfall' (*HT* 154).

It is during this game of Scrabble that the reader first discerns how completely Offred has been deprived of her senses, not her mental ones, but the physical sensations which most take for granted – touching, tasting, smelling, hearing, seeing. Deprived of these sensations by bland food, long covering garments, winged wimples and solitude, Offred assigns bizarre senses to ordinary objects or events. Though she initially thrills in *touching* the forbidden squares of the Scrabble game, eventually she wishes to *taste* and devour them: 'The counters are like candies, made of peppermint, cool like that. Humbugs, those were called. I would like to put them into my mouth. They would taste also of lime. The letter C. Crisp, slightly acid on the tongue, delicious' (*HT* 149).

This is not the first time Offred has invented sensory reactions which seem peculiar, but it is the first such extended passage, and thus more obvious. Earlier in the novel, Atwood has Offred connect the scent of nail polish with hunger (*HT* 39) and imagine she can smell Serena Joy's tears (*HT* 101). Later, Offred talks about 'the *stench* of [Serena's] knitting' (*HT* 109, italics mine), and, after the Birth Day ceremony, the smell of the other Wives' envy, 'faint wisps of acid, mingled with their perfume' (*HT* 136).

It seems that the only time when senses are connected to customary things is in Offred's memories, such as the time she imagines being with her daughter, breathing in 'baby powder and child's washed flesh and shampoo, with an undertone, the faint scent of urine' (*HT* 73), or when she is running away from bullets which sound 'sharp and crisp like a dry branch snapping' (*HT* 85). Similarly, when she is attempting escape with her family, she feels 'white, flat, thin' (*HT* 95), all of which could describe what her strained physical appearance would suggest. Later, when she is entrapped within Gilead, her metaphors become stranger: 'This is what I feel like: the sound of glass. I feel like the word *shatter*' (*HT* 113, italics in original).

The only other time when senses are connected with expected things comes when the senses are used as objective correlatives. For example, Offred notes that the bodies which hang on display, reminding residents of Gilead of the Commanders' powers and desire to rid the community of dissidents and traitors, are not left up there long in the summer because of the smell: 'This was once the land of air sprays, Pine and Floral, and people retain the taste; especially the Commanders, who preach purity in all things' (*HT* 174). Roberta Rubenstein believes that this passage recalls the idiom 'Cleanliness is next to Godliness' (Rubenstein in Van Spanckeren and Castro 108). It can also be used to show the fact that rot still exists in Gilead, just as air fresheners can only mask the odours, not kill them. Similarly, there is a smell attached to the Commander – mothballs (*HT* 106). This implies not only that he is old, but that the protection he and the other Commanders claim to give women in this new regime can only come at a cost.

This, then, is the sensory deprivation with which the protagonist lives. Offred's vision is cut off in this novel by the wings of the wimple she wears on her head and her circumscribed existence. Thus, what she can hear remains the most important way of learning about her predicament, but even then she can rarely trust what she is told. For Offred, knowledge that a resistance movement is out there is enough – she does not pursue direct contact with it. To some extent, she even resists it, especially once she falls in love with Nick and stops giving Ofglen the information she wants. Offred reveals, 'Ofglen is giving up on me. She whispers less, talks more about the weather. I do not feel regret about this. I feel relief' (*HT* 283).

Atwood characterizes Offred in this way in order to reinforce her non-heroic status, her everywoman position, her failure and her fears. Yet despite her passivity, Offred continues with her story and imagines a future audience:

> Dear *You*, I'll say. Just *you*, without a name. Attaching a name attaches *you* to the world of fact, which is riskier, more hazardous: who knows what the chances are out there, of survival, yours? I will say *you*, *you*, like an old love song. *You* can mean more than one.
>
> (*HT* 50, italics in original)

That the other half of her conversation is initially held with a man who does not heed her warning about forgiveness only makes her message more poignant for the reader, for the final words belong not to Offred, but to a future historian who transcribes, orders and tries to reconstruct her story. Mostly, he bemoans her ignorance: 'many gaps remain. Some of them could have been filled by our anonymous author, had she had a different turn of mind' (*HT* 322). He comes perilously close to forgiving the Gileadeans, attempting to suggest that any judgement is culturally specific and thus best avoided, and so the academic jargon of historical analysis ends up standing in for connection with Offred and her story. She is at fault, once again, the reluctant storyteller, the one who cannot offer up the facts the historian so desires. The novel ends in

a reconstructed world, with Gilead swept away, and the handmaid's fate ultimately unknown, though her final words offer up some hope: 'And so I step up,
into the darkness within, or else the light' (*HT* 307).

Atwood moves away from futuristic fiction in her next novel, *Cat's Eye*
(1988), which is often read as semi-autobiographical. *Cat's Eye* delineates post-
war urban Toronto and the mores of growing up female at a time when femininity was carefully regulated and scrutinized – as much by other women as it
was by men. *Cat's Eye* is by no means Atwood's most famous novel, but it was
deeply controversial when it appeared, given that its 'truths' could appear to
be antifeminist in nature. At the same time, the novel reflected an unmined
arena of women's lives, where their relationships with other women, and not a
'significant other' formed them more completely. The novel was published to
reviews that suggested both that feminism had come of age, and that antifem-
inism was alive and well. Such varied reactions are perhaps not surprising,
given the fact that the nature of truth is under debate in the novel as a whole, as
the first-person narrator remembers – and misremembers – her youth. Elaine
Risley takes the reader on a journey through contemporary Toronto and her
memories of growing up, weaving past and present skilfully throughout, and
offering more than one perspective – as befits the visual artist that she is. The
novel focuses on the position of the female artist (a recurring topic in Atwood's
oeuvre) as well as the myth of feminine solidarity, a myth taken apart at every
stage, from girlhood to adolescence to middle-aged adulthood.

In fact, Atwood herself thought that it was 'risky business' to focus on the
cruelty of little girls to each other (Ingersoll 2006, 121), a theme that features
heavily in the novel. Although, for a long period, Elaine represses memories
of her torment at the hands of Cordelia and other friends, she nevertheless
understands the legacy of those days when she considers her own daughters'
lives and has concern for what goes on behind closed doors: 'Little girls are
cute and small only to adults. To one another they are not cute. They are life-
sized' (*CE* 118). This radical revisioning of childhood goes further than the
torment of Brownies and dance classes in *Lady Oracle*, and touches on the
secrecy attached to girls' play.

Howells suggests that the novel 'could be read as Atwood's own retrospective glance back at the imaginative territory of her earlier fictions' (Howells
2005, 110) and it does seem that several issues get revisited: not only rituals of
childhood, but also the position of artists; women feeling ill at ease with other
women; and the spectre of feminism (and possibly postfeminism, too).

Elaine herself comes across as antifeminist at times, particularly when she
reflects on the fact that her first retrospective is at Sub-Versions, 'an alternative gallery run by a bunch of women' (*CE* 15). This is despite the fact that her

first real success came in just such an alternative venue. However, as the novel progresses, the reader sees more clearly the reasons for Elaine's fear of other women, and the deforming effects this has had on her life:

> I avoid gatherings of these women, walking as I do in fear of being sanctified, or else burned at the stake. I think they are talking about me, behind my back. They make me more nervous than ever, because they have a certain way they want me to be, and I am not that way. They want to improve me. At times I feel defiant: what right have they to tell me what to think? I am not Woman, and I'm damned if I'll be shoved into it. *Bitch*, I think silently. *Don't boss me around*   (*CE* 379, italics in original).

It is only when the reader understands that her induction into femininity and girlhood consisted of being always in the wrong, always improved upon, that this almost violent reaction to other women becomes understandable.

Some critics have connected Elaine's apparent misogyny to Atwood herself, as if her character is a mouthpiece for herself. Perhaps in some aspects she is, though it would be wrong to align them completely. There is, however, a very real sense that the crotchety Elaine being interviewed by the young female journalist during her retrospective exhibit is a thinly veiled self-portrait, given that Elaine refuses to offer easy answers to the journalist who wants to create a story about her influences and who wants to place her in a female continuum. As for feminism, Elaine snaps: '"I'm too old to have invented it and you're too young to understand it, so what's the point of discussing it at all?"' (*CE* 90). Atwood herself claims not to be a feminist – or perhaps more importantly, she claims a variety of stances towards feminism, including being belatedly embraced by the second-wave feminist movement. She challenges an easy equation of feminism and women, and she is as reluctant to be aligned with feminism as she is with any critical movement.

The novel explores 1950s Canada, the regulation of gender and gendered behaviour, the failure of the individual to understand herself, and the many interpretations of both art and autobiography. Here, art as visual art and art as literary art are very much connected; both are read – or misread – in a variety of ways. It is through remembering her past that Elaine tries to connect with the present, but, throughout, it is clear that memory itself is subject to reconstruction – just as the body, and femininity, too, are subject to manipulation.

Elaine is initiated into the cult of femininity once her unconventional family settles down in Toronto, and she learns to behave like a girl. The fact that her behaviour is learned and not innate is a clear example of how socialization reifies behaviour, or makes what is constructed seem natural. She acquires two schoolfriends, Carol Campbell and Grace Smeath, both of whom come from conventional families. In attempting to belong to their world, she notes: 'Playing with girls is different and at first I feel strange as I do it, self-conscious, as if I'm only doing an imitation of a girl. But I soon get used to it' (*CE* 52). What she becomes, in this new role, is a consumer; what she lets go of is her competitive nature, a nature fuelled by growing up with an older brother.

> I begin to want things I've never wanted before: braids, a dressing-gown, a purse of my own. Something is unfolding, being revealed to me. I see that there's a whole world of girls and their doings that has been unknown to me, and that I can be part of it without making any effort at all. I don't have to keep up with anyone, run as fast, aim as well, make loud explosive noises, decode messages, die on cue. I don't have to think about whether I've done these things well, as well as a boy. All I have to do is sit on the floor and cut frying pans out of the Eaton's Catalogue with embroidery scissors, and say I've done it badly. Partly this is a relief.   (*CE* 54)

This willed inertia is disturbing, as is the sense that accomplishment must be left to the boys. Elaine's relief at not having to succeed is short-lived, however, because after a summer away, she returns to find that a new girl has infiltrated her group of friends: Cordelia. Cordelia becomes the enforcer of behaviour, and Elaine's judge, so much so that she loses any confidence she had in herself or her body: '*What do you have to say for yourself?* Cordelia used to ask. *Nothing*, I would say. It was a word I came to connect with myself, as if I was nothing, as if there was nothing there at all' (*CE* 41, italics in original). Elaine begins surreptitiously to peel skin off her fingers and feet, to mutilate herself in order to fit in, but she never measures up to Cordelia's standards of behaviour, which vary enough day by day to leave Elaine always unsure of herself.

Cordelia brings mirrors to school to shame Elaine, repeating the regulating and controlling phrase, ' "Look at yourself! Just look!" ' (*CE* 158). If in *The Handmaid's Tale*, constant surveillance is required to keep control, so it is in *Cat's Eye*, where Elaine learns to internalize the controlling gaze. Atwood here is playing with the idea of the panopticon, a kind of prison designed to offer apparently constant surveillance of the inmates and thereby control their antisocial behaviour. The theory of the panopticon, explicated by Michel Foucault in *Discipline and Punish*, is that by shielding the inspector from the prisoners, the inspector maintains power: inmates have no choice but to assume that they are always being watched, with the result that they regulate their own behaviour. Foucault notes:

> Hence the major effect of the Panopticon: to induce in the inmate a state of conscious and permanent visibility that assures the automatic functioning of power. So to arrange things that the surveillance is

permanent in its effects, even if it is discontinuous in its action: that the perfection of power should tend to render its actual exercise unnecessary.   (Foucault 201)

Cordelia maintains her power through offers of friendship, revoked; none of the girls knows whom Cordelia will torment next, only that there will be a next time. They vie with each other not to be the victim, and this constant need to measure up haunts Elaine throughout her life.

Molly Hite argues that Atwood shows that female anxiety is rooted in the internalization of 'a permanent belief in her need for improvement, a belief essential to her primary role as consumer, as the magazine advertisements indicate' (Hite 142). Certainly, Elaine does internalize this (particularly when she cuts out photographs or pictures of women fighting stains or bodily imperfections), and these early lessons colour all subsequent relationships with women. They also affect her subsequent art, as she concentrates on paintings of women and domestic appliances. Hite argues that the novel as a whole concerns 'visibility: about who sees and is seen, about evading or controlling the gaze, about the seeing that is the precondition and product of art' (Hite 136); thus Elaine's life story and her art are firmly connected – in an interesting twist on Atwood's stance about the separability of art and life. Intriguingly, Elaine herself does not see the connections between her work and her biography – though the reader does. Thus, blindness is just as important as sight and visibility in the novel.

Elaine's torment comes to an abrupt halt when a prank goes too far and she is nearly killed. Forced to go down into the ravine to retrieve a hat that Cordelia threw down there in order to punish Elaine for laughing at her, Elaine slips through the ice into the freezing water and barely makes it home. At one point, it seems that she will give up, but she sees a vision of the Virgin Mary, who helps her to find the strength. After this, Elaine discovers an inner power and no longer has any dealings with the other children. She represses her memories of this time so effectively that when Cordelia re-enters her life after a period away (having failed at a private school), Elaine does not acknowledge their past, and she is confused by her mother's hesitation over the friendship. She also takes on some of Cordelia's bullying characteristics, and her 'mean mouth': 'The person I use my mean mouth on most is Cordelia. She doesn't even have to provoke me, I use her as target practice' (*CE* 235). Cordelia and Elaine have swapped places, but both need the other for their aggressive performances, performances that both take on board femininity (they are ruthlessly cruel to others and their failings) and disregard it. Elaine eventually goes to art school and eschews most feminine accoutrements, whereas Cordelia might be said to take her femininity too far: into hysteria. She is sent to a private rest home following a suicide attempt. From this point on, she only really recurs as a haunting presence – and particularly as the one viewer to Elaine's retrospective who never arrives. Elaine longs for Cordelia's presence: 'If I were to meet Cordelia again, what would I tell her about myself? The truth, or whatever would make me look good? Probably the latter. I still have that need' (*CE* 6). As at least a partially self-aware narrator, Elaine offers the reader some truths, but reserves others; here, the reader needs to work actively to fill in the gaps, and to see what even Elaine refuses to see.

What comes back over and over in this novel is how the adult Elaine misremembers her childhood, so much so that she cannot recognize the genesis of her own paintings. *Falling Women*, for example, she reads as being related to men: 'Fallen women were women who had fallen onto men and hurt themselves. There was some suggestion of downward motion, against one's will and not with the will of anyone else. Fallen women were not pulled-down women or pushed women, merely fallen' (*CE* 268). Yet her painting is entitled *Falling Women* and not *Fallen Women*, and depicts three women falling off a bridge, as if by accident (*CE* 268), replicating her own fear of the bridge, the ravine and the three girls who tormented her there.

Elaine exhibits her collection of Mrs Smeath paintings, one of which has a bottle of ink thrown over it, and this transforms her own thoughts about her work (as it does for others): 'I will be looked at, now, with respect: paintings that can get bottles of ink thrown at them, that can inspire such outraged violence, such uproar and display, must have an odd revolutionary power. I will seem audacious, and brave. Some dimension of heroism has been added to me' (*CE* 354). Again, the need to be seen from the outside is foregrounded here.

Finally, a series of six paintings, 'Pressure Cooker', about her mother, is read through several different lenses: some read the work as offering earth-goddess imagery, others as female slavery, but Elaine insists, 'it was only my mother cooking, in the ways and places she used to cook, in the late forties' (*CE* 151). However, it is significant that she recounts how much her mother did not like cooking, and how she painted it just after her mother died. In relation to other domestic appliances that she obsessively paints, Elaine muses, 'I have no image of myself in relation to them. They are suffused with anxiety, but it's not my own anxiety. The anxiety is in the things themselves' (*CE* 337). As readers, we are taken back to the cutting and pasting of items from a catalogue – the initiation rite through which Elaine learned how to behave like a girl, memories that the adult Elaine cannot access. Hite argues, 'The question of how to read these paintings is in many ways analogous to the question of how to read *Cat's Eye* as a whole' (Hite 138). In other words, is the art feminist or antifeminist; is domesticity celebrated or abjured? Elaine

Risley's retrospective exhibit rereads her artwork in a feminist framework, but perhaps it does this simply because it coincided with a rise in the feminist world view rather than a rise in Elaine's own viewpoint. In the end, Elaine suspects it does not matter: 'I can no longer control these paintings, or tell them what to mean. Whatever energy they have came out of me. I'm what's left over' (*CE* 409).

Elaine is a limited and unreliable narrator of her life, her paintings partially representing what she has repressed. The novel as a whole offers up an intriguing blend of apparent autobiography and art, and reveals influences of one on the other. What it does not do is offer any answers – another familiar Atwoodian motif.

In *The Robber Bride* (1993), Atwood manipulates the fairy tale and deals primarily with a woman's right to be bad. It is the first of Atwood's novels to be more explicitly identified with postfeminism (though *Cat's Eye* also makes a short reference to the critical position). It addresses some of the familiar concerns of feminism, but recasts them, often in comic ways. The novel does not deny feminism (indeed, much of the novel itself is taken up, obliquely, with critiquing feminism), but it does often signal a disassociation with it. For example, the idea of consumption that permeates many feminist novels of the early part of the second wave of the feminist movement (not least in Atwood's own first novel, *The Edible Woman*) is playfully re-enacted in *The Robber Bride*. It is also a novel explicitly about food and desire, with a comically monstrous woman at the centre – Zenia, a woman who appears in many guises but who never gets to tell her own story. Instead, she is seen through others, three female friends who are linked through their hatred of her after she steals each of their men in turn. In her own critical writing, Atwood has claimed that 'powerful, or at any rate active, heroes and villains are seen as the fulfillment of a *human* ideal; whereas powerful women … are usually given a supernatural power' (*SW* 223, author's italics). Zenia is so powerful in the novel that she actually comes back from the dead (or appears to), though she haunts the women even before this resurrection.

Analysing mythic constructions of monstrous women, Kim Chernin notes, 'These fearful she-monsters not only destroy men: they eat, they swallow, they suck. They are voracious. This image of woman as destructive seems inextricably involved with the idea of eating' (Chernin 131–2). Zenia becomes a maneater extraordinaire who is both heroine and villain of her own text. Atwood's humorous take on the role of the maneater is articulated by Roz, one of the trio of women who is first taken in by Zenia and then betrayed by her: 'Most women disapprove of man-eaters; not so much because of the activity itself, or the promiscuity involved, but because of the greed. Women don't want all the men eaten up by man-eaters; they want a few left over so they can eat some themselves' (*RB* 392).

At the heart of *The Robber Bride* lies an examination of the power of women, both as objects of desire, and as desiring subjects. In Atwood's novel, the devouring female is multiple: she is Zenia, the maneater who devours and then abandons three men; she is also Tony, Roz and Charis, the devoted women to whom these hapless men have been attached. It is striking how much emphasis is placed on food in the novel: food as nutrition, as absolution, as ceremony. This idea of ceremony is key, as we think of the place that Zenia occupies in the text. Is she real? Has she been 'raised from the dead'? Why *does* she apparently have so much power? Zenia, whether 'ghost' or 'real', haunts the women with whom she comes into contact, and in doing so, ensures that each woman recreates her past encounter with Zenia, and relives the personal past which allowed Zenia power.

The women of *The Robber Bride* epitomize various stances towards hunger, with Charis a near anorexic and Roz a compulsive overeater. Tony is associated with the preparation of food, something she learned, it appears, from Zenia. Tony is connected to 'safe' food, domestic food – tea, and cookies, tuna casserole and menus from *The Joy of Cooking* (not to be confused with *The Joy of Sex*). Indeed, when Tony lets Zenia into her life a second time, it is because she thinks the knock on the door signals Girl Guides selling cookies. The imagery that follows – lamb blood dripping on the floor from the skewer that Tony holds in her hand – is deliberately at odds with such home-based comforts. However, Tony herself has a taste for blood that is treated comically in order to defuse it. As a war historian, she recreates various battles on a sand table, and uses kitchen spices to represent the armies:

> Absent-mindedly she picks up one of Otto's fallen cloves, dips it into her glass of water to get rid of any hairspray, and pops it into her mouth. It's a bad habit of hers, eating parts of the armies on her map; luckily there are always replacements in the bottles on the spice shelves upstairs. But the dead soldiers would have been eaten, too, one way or another, or at least dismembered.   (*RB* 113)

Because Tony cannot acknowledge her own desire for bloodshed or power, she hides her desires behind the cloak of academic impenetrability. Yet her very hunger here betrays her; thus, the story Zenia makes up about her past in order to entice Tony into partnership is one of war and destruction.

For Charis, food is bland but necessary, healthy and vegetarian. She is the closest to Atwood's earlier anorexic heroine who sees food as a punishment. Indeed, it is through pretending to share Charis's disgust of food that Zenia gains power over her. Zenia claims to have left West because 'He tries to get me to eat … mounds of food, steak and butter, all those animal fats. They make me nauseated, I can't, I just can't!' (*RB* 221). Charis is what remains from Karen after she undergoes traumatic sexual abuse at the hands of her uncle, and her rejection of bodily presence includes both food and desire, linking back as she does to the stereotypical construction of the anorexic girl. However, Charis is not entirely unable to see that food, like sex, is pleasurable – for others. For one thing, she enjoys 'watch[ing] Roz eat French bread, cracking it open, burying her nose in it – *This is so good, this is so* good! – before sinking her firm white teeth into it' (*RB* 63, italics in original). For Charis, Zenia is the sexual woman she will not allow herself to be, and thus her own desire must be projected onto an Other, either malevolently or benignly.

Roz is the ultimate hungry woman, who diets and gorges, often almost simultaneously. Roz's incorporation of food is linked to comfort but also to fear of being found wanting, as well as to her guilty assumption of power; she is still in thrall to the idea of the woman as a feminine (and therefore petite) creature. Despite her inability to fulfil this role, she craves the kind of attention that only Zenia seems to attract. It is in contemplating the new, undead Zenia that Roz especially thinks of food – rotting vegetables or spicy 'foreign' food (*RB* 391). When she asks a private detective to follow Zenia, she instructs her to find out what Zenia has for breakfast, and this is not just an ironic nod to the detective genre. In business, Roz is said to have 'a gourmet's taste for the underbelly' (*RB* 94). When she contemplates the women with whom her cheating husband has sex, she pretends to think of them as no more than 'things', but her imagery is actually associated with food: they are 'cotton candy' (*RB* 300). She is particularly appalled that Mitch can 'just write these women off. Sink his teeth into them, spit them out, and Roz is expected to clean up the mess' (*RB* 298). It is only fitting, therefore, that this wolfish figure is himself eventually consumed and regurgitated. Indeed, Roz herself imagines Mitch 'thrown from the troika, thrown to the wolves, to the hordes of ravening bimbos snapping at his heels' (*RB* 300). She has no immediate wish to save him: 'she … want[s] a little blood, just a drop or two, because she's thirsty' (*RB* 375). In this, she is not so different from Zenia herself.

It is not by accident that when Zenia is resurrected from the dead, the other women see her first in a restaurant named Toxique: the foreign as toxic, the toxic as Other. Zenia is what the women wish to be but cannot: vampish and vampiric. Tony imagines her thus: 'Maybe her teeth are in [West's] neck, right now; maybe she's sucking his life's blood while Tony sits here … not even knowing where to look, because Zenia could be anywhere, she could be doing anything, and so far Tony doesn't have a clue' (*RB* 408). Zenia may be the archetypal maneater, but the other women refuse to recognize what she represents within themselves. Moreover, while the women are, in a way, both hunted and haunted by Zenia, they survive; it is the men who falter: Charis's boyfriend Billy disappears for good; Roz's husband Mitch commits suicide. Tony's husband West goes to Zenia and returns, each time shattered by the experience: '*He's small game*, pleads Tony silently. *A tiny fish. Why bother?* But Zenia likes hunting. She likes hunting anything. She relishes it' (*RB* 37, italics in original). The metaphors for hunting and fishing abound. Billy is 'too small a catch'; men are 'target practice'. Tony even goes so far as to imagine that Zenia 'has a row of men's dicks nailed to her wall, like stuffed animal heads' (*RB* 281). While not quite the image of a cannibal, this fantasy of Tony's suggests Zenia's place as a hunter who takes prizes.

Zenia is a difficult character whose identity is posited as both fantastic and real, and critics disagree over her final 'positive' or 'negative' role. Yet to assign her a space which marks her off as one or another thing is to fall into the realistic fallacy which suggests that female characters are representative of social rights or wrongs; it also harks back to an earlier stage of feminist criticism that attempted to applaud or reject characters based on their assumed alliance to women's emancipation. Donna Potts, for example, argues that Zenia is trapped into conforming to stereotypical positions (Potts 297), but this is a misreading of Zenia, who self-consciously adopts those positions and co-opts them, and who may never even exist on the same plane as Charis, Roz and Tony anyway. Atwood deconstructs easy critical positions when she places Zenia outside the realm of good versus bad. Zenia is, we must remember, first introduced to us as a ghost.

It is not possible finally to assign clear roles to any of Atwood's characters, and feminism itself is a contested programme in *The Robber Bride*, coming up in unexpected and not entirely comfortable ways. For Roz, feminism is an outgrown phase, signified by overalls and body hair and replaced, albeit uncomfortably, with sleek, shoulder-padded business women. For Tony, it is a battle she does not wish to enter, in part because she thinks it will mean that her interest in war will be cast out as not properly feminist. The most she will do is blandly read the graffiti in the women's toilet about the battle between history and women's studies: 'Herstory not History … Hesterectromy not Hysterectomy … Historic not Herstoric … Omens of a coming tussle Tony hopes to avoid' (*RB* 25). Feminism seems to have passed Charis by entirely. It is significant that only Zenia consistently uses the rhetoric of feminism and its stereotypical consciousness-raising sharing – and only to her own ends: personal power. As J. Brooks Bouson argues, 'Zenia fabricates a story about her own victimization because she recognizes the power and prestige associated with the victim role' (Bouson 1995, 154). Contrasting Naomi Wolf's versions of victim feminism and power feminism, Bouson suggests that Zenia makes use of whatever stance will best assist her in a particular moment, and the switch between them is dizzying and contrived.

Female power is *not* benevolent, Atwood suggests, in her comic reworking of Gothic fairy tale in which women's hunger is powerful and possessive. Clearly, the evil woman/good woman binary opposition does not hold in *The Robber Bride*, something which Roz's twin daughters make particularly clear. As children, they go through a phase of wanting every storybook character to be female: 'The Big Bad Wolf fell down the chimney, right into the cauldron of boiling water, and got his fur all burned off. *Her* fur! It's odd what a difference it makes, changing the pronoun' (*RB* 294). They 'opt for women in every single role' (*RB* 294).

Zenia's predatory nature is not new – 'evil' women, powerful women, have filled the pages of many a literary text, and, like Zenia, they often come to a 'bad end'; Zenia is, after all, dead a second time at the end of the novel. But what about Charis, Roz and Tony? They, too, are powerful women, and if they are not quite so aggressive in their pursuit, they also entertain wildly violent fantasies of control. Yet in their very proximity to the voracious women of myths and legends, it may be that they are reclaiming spaces that women have perhaps been denied – even by feminism itself.

In *Alias Grace* (1996), Atwood creates her most famous 'villainess' to date, going even further in her depiction of female bad behaviour than she did in constructing Zenia. Atwood based her novel on the historical Grace Marks, a young Irish immigrant servant who was convicted of murdering her employer Thomas Kinnear in Canada and who was sent to Kingston prison for life (she also spent some time in a lunatic asylum, where she was on display to paying visitors, as Susanna Moodie famously noted). James McDermott, who was also convicted of the crime, was hanged, and Grace became a cause célèbre amongst individuals who did not believe that women could be capable of such monstrosity. Kinnear's housekeeper Nancy Montgomery was also murdered but neither Marks nor McDermott was tried for that crime. Eventually, the historical Marks was pardoned after thirty years in prison and disappeared from the historical record, and Atwood was scrupulous in her historiography in never deviating from known fact, as she recounts in her article 'In Search of Alias Grace':

> I devised the following set of guidelines for myself: when there was
> a solid fact, I could not alter it; long as I might to have Grace witness
> James McDermott's execution, it could not be done, because, worse
> luck, she was already in the penitentiary on that day. Also, every major

element in the book had to be suggested by something in the writing about Grace and her times, however dubious such writing might be; but, in the parts left unexplained – the gaps left unfilled – I was free to invent. Since there were a lot of gaps, there is a lot of invention.   (227)

The novel is clearly a work of fictionalized history, and, in it, Grace takes on multiple roles. The text is a multiple narrative made up of many voices and textual styles, and, within it, Atwood includes letters, epigraphs and ballads as frames around different sections, all of which are also framed by a quilting motif. Each of the potential explanations for Grace's behaviour (or the events surrounding the murders) is advanced (and then retreated from): that she is bad, and really a criminal who deserved her punishment; that she is mad, and not responsible for her crime; that she was McDermott's unwilling accomplice and dupe; that she herself was in love with more than one man, including potentially both McDermott and Kinnear and therefore the main force behind the events. Atwood skilfully weaves together these multiple stories and multiple voices: not only of Grace, but of the men who try to understand her, including Simon Jordan, an American doctor who, sixteen years after the event, tries to get her to use word association in order to uncover whether she truly does have the complete amnesia that she claims; Dr Jerome DuPont, a hypnotist and con man, who is also known to Grace as the itinerant peddler Jeremiah; Jamie Walsh, the boy whose evidence helps convict her (and whom she later marries); and Reverend Verringer, who also wants to find out the truth.

As ever, truth is tricky and elusive, and the reader is never fully satisfied, though a fantastic potential truth is revealed near the end of the novel. However, Atwood withholds just enough to make the reader question this potential truth; she even discounts an earlier version of the story that she herself penned. In the Author's Afterword, Atwood writes:

> The story of the Kinnear murders has been fictionalized twice before: as *A Master Killing*, by Ronald Hambleton (1978), which concerns itself mainly with the pursuit of the suspects; and by Margaret Atwood, in the CBC television play *The Servant Girl* (1974, directed by George Jonas), which relied exclusively on the Moodie version and cannot now be taken as definitive.   (*AG* 469)

Indeed, there is no definitive version offered. It is a novel that has been considered a mosaic (Christie March), or based on quilting metaphors (Howells, Sharon Wilson and Jennifer Murray, amongst others) or a novel about language (Lorna Hutchison), class position (Sandra Kumamoto Stanley), or the truth that resides (or does not) in written documentation (Judith Knelman).

Atwood herself claims, 'If you're after the truth, the whole and detailed truth, and nothing but the truth, you're going to have a thin time of it if you trust to paper; but, with the past, it's almost all you've got' (*CP* 225).

The novel begins with an apparent recollection of Grace's, about Nancy, which blends her experiences of confinement in the prison, her memories of the first day she was in service at the Kinnear residence and the hope that she could change the pattern of events so that Nancy and Kinnear remained alive. It is based on the eighth year of her imprisonment, and the two-page passage effectively meshes together all of the events of the book, and ends with a one-line paragraph: 'This is what I told Dr. Jordan, when we came to that part of the story' (*AG* 6). Thus, Atwood casts doubt on what Grace says early on. After all, she also notes, when she first meets Dr Jordan, 'Perhaps I will tell you lies' (*AG* 41) and there is a firm emphasis placed on stories throughout – not only the stories Grace tells Simon, but the stories each tells each other, from the stories of murders 'collected' by Grace's mistress, the Prison Governor's wife, to the stories Dr Jordan tells about himself – as well as about the women with whom he comes into contact. He thinks that 'one must present what ought to be true as if it really is' (*AG* 87), particularly when it comes to the refined nature of women, in which he would like to believe, even as he dabbles in sexual adventures and fantasies that strip women of their refinement.

Howells suggests that the men who wish to rescue Grace in some way, including Dr Jordan, 'share a fascination with the possibility of Grace's sexual transgressions, just as they share the same strangely ambivalent trait of refusing to let Grace speak for herself or of not understanding what she does say' (Howells 2003, 36). Certainly it is the case that Grace recognizes that her role as servant makes her vulnerable sexually – her friend Mary Whitney, for example, dies as a result of a botched abortion after an affair with the son of the household for which they both work, and Grace suggests that this story of sexual betrayal is a familiar one, re-enacted too frequently. In this way, women's stories revolve around men, and men define them: even Simon Jordan says, 'His father was self-made, but his mother was constructed by others, and such edifices are notoriously fragile' (*AG* 56).

Grace recognizes that her position as servant (and now prisoner) affords her some freedoms. Having never been a lady, she muses that she can 'say anything I like; or if I don't wish to, I needn't say anything at all' (*AG* 90). Moreover, she can see more clearly than a lady can:

> There is a good deal that can be seen slantwise, especially by the ladies, who do not wish to be caught staring. They can also see through veils, and window curtains, and over the tops of fans; and it is a good thing they can see in this way, or they would never see much of anything. But

those of us who do not have to be bothered with all the veils and fans manage to see a good deal more.   (*AG* 229)

Yet Grace is not unaware of the need for pretence herself, and in her stories, she selects carefully the details that will tantalize him, withholding from him (though often not from the reader) the particularly interesting parts: 'As long as I say something, anything at all, Dr. Jordan smiles and writes it down, and tells me I am doing well' (*AG* 69).

In an effort to reignite her memory, he offers her root vegetables, hoping that they will remind her of the cellar and thus what happened when Nancy Montgomery died, but Grace deflects him by offering cooking tips. When he wants to know more about her dreams, she does not always tell him, arguing, 'Just because he pesters me to know everything is no reason for me to tell him' (*AG* 216). Moreover, she argues, 'I have little enough of my own, no belongings, no possessions, no privacy to speak of, and I need to keep something for myself; and in any case, what use would he have for my dreams, after all?' (*AG* 101).

At times, his questioning of her reminds her of the courtroom, where she realized that 'every word that came out of my mouth was as if burnt into the paper they were writing it on, and once I said a thing I knew I could never get the words back; only they were the wrong words, because whatever I said would be twisted around, even if it was the plain truth in the first place' (*AG* 68). Howells suggests that the novel 'tells history from a feminine perspective, challenging and resisting the discourses of masculine authority which con-stitute official historical accounts' (Howells 2005, 140). After all, Grace does elude Simon Jordan's grasp; she avoids the death penalty originally handed down; and she never quite offers up that final truth. Atwood argues that Grace is formed by two contradictory motives: to 'narrate' and to 'withhold', and that 'the only power left to her as a convicted and imprisoned criminal comes from a blend of these two motives' (*CP* 227). It is a power she wields carefully. She is like Scheherazade, as her lawyer suggests, arguing that she has the right in her stories not to be 'subjected to the harsh categories of Truth and Falsehood' (*AG* 377); and she is also like Penelope, who weaves and waits. She uses particularly feminine arts: quilting, stitching and dressmaking around which to thread her stories. Howells argues, 'Atwood's appropriation of traditional patchwork art highlights her postmodern reconstruction of history, which is presented here as a "patchwork" of conflicting evidence from which the reader has to arrange a meaningful design' (Howells 2005, 153).

Near the end of the novel, in a chapter entitled 'Pandora's Box', Grace is apparently hypnotized by Dr Jerome DuPont, with Simon as a witness; what happens next thrills all who witness it. Grace appears to take on another's voice, and another's demeanour. As Simon notes bewildered, 'This voice cannot be

Grace's; yet in that case, whose voice is it?' (*AG* 400). This is a crucial question, one that could be asked of the novel as a whole. The voice claims, '"I am not Grace! Grace knew nothing about it!"' (*AG* 401).

At the end of the performance, Grace is led away, and the gathered men begin to discuss what has happened; Reverend Verringer believes that it was a case of possession, by Grace's friend Mary Whitney; DuPont claims to be perplexed by the event; Simon Jordan suggests that the answer is a neurological event (*AG* 405). It leaves Jordan uneasy: 'What happened in the library? Was Grace really in a trance, or was she play-acting, and laughing up her sleeve? He knows what he saw and heard, but he may have been shown an illusion, which he cannot prove to have been one' (*AG* 407).

Atwood herself claims, 'Truth is sometimes unknowable, at least by us' (*CP* 228). Instead of attempting to record the night's events, Simon returns briskly to the USA, then to Europe, and is last observed having been severely injured in the American Civil War, his wits lost.

The novel concludes with Grace ensconced in domesticity: married to Jamie Walsh and possibly expecting a child. The conclusion of the novel therefore resembles a generic nineteenth-century closure, as Grace's individual story is subsumed in the larger one of marriage. The warden's daughter, on hearing of the release, cries melodramatically, a response Grace finds bemusing: 'when I asked her why she was doing that, she said it was because I was to have a happy ending, and it was just like a book; and I wondered what books she'd been reading' (*AG* 443). However, this 'happy ending' is undercut through ways that the domestic space resembles and reflects the space of the prison, and the way in which her husband constantly forces her to re-enact a form of penance. In this reading she is never really free after all.

Atwood's first book of the new millennium, *The Blind Assassin* (2000), was a novel looking back at Canadian history, particularly in relation to the 1930s and 1940s, and revealing the detrimental effects of class and gender division. It is also a book about celebrity, and the consequences of rash actions on individuals and families, as well as an experiment in genre and style. It incorporates newspaper reports, snippets of what becomes a famous novel, and stories that at first are hard to place and understand. It begins with the death of Laura Chase, the sister of Iris Chase Griffen. We hear Iris's voice from the first page, but she is replaced by other voices until the start of section three, when she returns as a first-person narrator. *The Blind Assassin* is also the name of the novel ascribed to Laura, though later found to be written by Iris herself. Iris manipulates the truth, manufactures her dead sister's celebrity and conceals herself behind it, writing snide letters to academics who wish to know more about Laura as well as to fans who recapitulate the image of the suicidal female writer whose art takes precedence over life. It is ironic that as the novel becomes more famous – the singular text of a doomed writer – it no longer brings in any revenue to Iris, since she has chosen not to be identified as the author and the copyright has thus run out. Iris bemoans the fact that 'you lose control. The thing is out there in the world, replicating itself in God knows how many forms, without the say-so from me' (*BA* 283); yet she has given up (or never asserted) authorship, and her publication of the novel is both a memorial to her sister and her lover Alex Thomas, and a form of revenge against her husband Richard, who sexually abused both Iris and Laura.

In the present tense of the novel, Iris is an octogenarian woman trying to set the record straight before she dies. She is querulous, lonely and unlikeable, with a fierce tongue and a desire to create havoc wherever she goes. Attending a graduation ceremony at a local school, and presenting a prize in commemoration of what everyone believes is her sister's posthumously published novel, Iris bends towards the young female recipient and says, '*Bless you. Be careful. Anyone intending to meddle with words needs such blessing, such warning*' (*BA* 41, italics in original). It is a warning she does not heed herself, and in this second version of her life, Iris tries to explore the motivations for writing as well as the process of writing itself. It is something she puzzles over and reworks throughout the narrative: 'For whom am I writing this? For myself? I think not. I have no picture of myself reading it over at a later time, *later time* having become problematical. For some stranger, in the future, after I'm dead? I have no such ambition, or no such hope' (*BA* 43, italics in original). Later, she imagines Myra, her former housekeeper's daughter and present carer, reading it; though if she does write for Myra, Iris reinforces her reputation for being harsh if not vindictive in that she both complains about Myra's taste and appearance, and mischievously suggests that they may be half-sisters. Finally, she claims to write for Sabrina, her missing granddaughter, from whom she is estranged; and critics claim that the final novel, which is an amalgamation of Iris's memoirs, excerpts from 'Laura's' novel and newspaper clippings of public events in Iris's life (including the death announcements of her sister, daughter, husband, sister-in-law and finally herself) is compiled and published by Sabrina in the end, though Sabrina never figures in the present tense of the novel at all, and is only a fleeting presence – like Aimee, her mother – in the overall narrative. Howells argues that within the novel, 'The reader's attention is insistently drawn to the different conventions through which stories may be told, so that the interaction between them is a constant reminder of the artifice of storytelling' (Howells 2005, 156). Certainly the narratives are woven together in a way that causes the reader to pause and re-evaluate what is being said and why as well as whose perspective is offered. Iris herself suggests, 'The only way you can write the truth is to assume that what you set down will never be read. Not by any other person, and not even by yourself at some later date. Otherwise you begin excusing yourself' (*BA* 283). Yet at other times, she does reread her work, and berates herself for what is there – and what is missing.

> I've looked back over what I've set down so far, and it seems inadequate. Perhaps there's too much frivolity in it, or too many things that might be taken for frivolity. A lot of clothes, the styles and colours outmoded now, shed butterflies' wings. A lot of dinners, not always very good ones. Breakfasts, picnics, ocean voyages, costume balls, newspapers, boating on the river. Such items do not assort very well with tragedy. But in life, tragedy is not one long scream. It includes everything that led up to it.
>
> (*BA* 417)

If it is not one long scream, it is certainly a whimper of pain, or even at times, a howl. Iris claims about Laura, 'But some people can't tell where it hurts. They can't calm down. They can't ever stop howling' (*BA* 2). As if to understand and situate this pain, Iris recreates it, picking over the past as if it is a scab that has not healed.

The novel looks back to Iris's childhood as the daughter of a button-factory owner; she is mostly seen in relation to others (later, she is viewed as the wife of the industrialist Richard Griffen). Iris's mother died after a miscarriage when Iris was young, and she feels confined by her mother's dying wish that she should take care of Laura, whatever happens. This role is one that Iris both tries to fulfil and wilfully abandons, depending on her mood, and on Laura's behaviour. Laura is an odd child, who unsettles those around her with her views about God and sacrifice, and her unwillingness to live a conventional life or to recognize that she is supposed to behave with propriety. Iris later considers that Laura's behaviour is unsettling precisely because she does what others would like to do, but are afraid to; she exhibits what they keep hidden. Yet she is also a puzzle of sorts, or as J. Brooks Bouson claims, a 'textual enigma' (Bouson 2003, 252). Bouson claims that as a mute trauma victim (for Laura is sexually assaulted by at least two men in the novel, and reacts with extreme passivity, even withdrawal, both times), she is 'Iris's shadow self and spiritual collaborator' (252).

It is certainly the case that they are intimately linked, not only through kinship, but also because they both fall in love with the same man, Alex Thomas, whom they meet at a public picnic. A photograph of Alex with the two sisters is published in the papers, and Laura steals the original and makes two prints of it, one for Iris and one for herself. In her doctored versions, however, Alex is pictured alone with each of the sisters; only a stray hand that cannot be cropped out betrays the truth. Thus, Laura recognizes, if even perhaps Iris does not, that their triangular relationship requires a forced revisioning of reality. In Laura's picture, it is Iris's hand that remains, and in Iris's version, Laura's hand is revealed. This is symbolically important, because the photograph reappears at crucial points in the novel: near the beginning, when it is part of 'Laura's' novel; in the recollection of the picnic itself; and in the epilogue, where the novel's beginnings are rewritten, with a twist. As the narrator of the epilogue reveals, 'The picture is of happiness, the story not. Happiness is a garden walled with glass: there's no way in or out. In Paradise there are no stories, because there are no journeys. It's loss and regret and misery and yearning that drive the story forward, along its twisted road' (*BA* 518). Certainly there is no happy ending in store for any of the principal characters, and love does not save them.

Alex is a young Communist agitator and writer who may or may not have been involved in setting fire to their father's factory and precipitating the Chase family downfall. Iris and Laura hide the young man in their attic, an act that Iris first sees as her way of helping Laura, and later recognizes as her own desire for Alex herself. Yet he slips away from the narrative as the Chase family's future is placed in doubt as a result of the fire, only to return later and set up further destruction. The family's financial ruin results in Iris's ill-fated marriage to Richard Griffen, a man who represents 'new money' and who marries Iris not only for her youth (she is eighteen to his thirty-five), but also for the connections she might bring, and for the façade of respectability the marriage might confer. Iris agrees to the marriage to save her family home and to protect Laura, but the marriage actually ensures the destruction of both. Moreover, shortly after they marry, her father dies, and her new husband keeps this knowledge from her in order not to spoil their honeymoon – but mostly to keep her under control. His method of withholding information from his wife continues throughout their marriage, particularly in relation to her family. He is also a sexual bully who delights in harming her:

> I sometimes felt as if these marks on my body were a kind of code, which blossomed, then faded, like invisible ink held to a candle. But if they were a code, who held the key to it?
>
> I was sand, I was snow – written on, rewritten, smoothed over.
>
> (*BA* 371)

Iris cannot read her situation because she has blindly entered her marriage and has no female companions against whom to compare her life; her sister-in-law Winifred is aligned firmly with Richard (and even colludes in his treatment of Laura); her father's mistress Callista is too young to want a clear role in her life; and Reenie, the housekeeper who helped raise her, spouts conventional views about women's roles. Bouson argues that the novel revolves around 'women's cultural blindness to, and thus collusion with, their own victimization as well as the victimization of other women' (Bouson 2003, 251). In fact, only the otherworldly Laura recognizes what is in store for Iris, and that she is entering into a trap. But at this point (and at others) Iris values security more than freedom, and thus she does not take up Laura's offer of escape into a different class (running away and working as a waitress). Iris is blind not only to her own situation, but to that of Laura, who is repeatedly raped by Richard. Laura becomes pregnant and, to avoid a scandal, Richard spirits her away, claiming she had a breakdown. She is forced to undergo an abortion and is kept apart from Iris, who shamefully does not try too hard to see her because she is afraid that Laura will work out that Iris is having an affair with Alex, who is the father of her daughter Aimee. Reenie does eventually attempt to save Laura, though she seems to regard Iris as having made her own choices. At this point, the sisters are severed from each other for a number of years, only to be reunited shortly before Laura's death.

Iris's secret relationship with Alex is outlined in the interpolated novel *The Blind Assassin*, though readers wrongly assume that the novel depicts Laura's affair with an unnamed man. Iris knows that the novel's reputation is based in part on salacious gossip about Laura, and reflects that in publishing it, 'I did believe, at first, that I wanted only justice. I thought my heart was pure. We do like to have such good opinions of our own motives when we're about to do something harmful, to someone else' (*BA* 497). What is key here is that the relationship Iris reveals is not wholly romantic; Alex (or the man referred to only as 'he') is brutal to the woman in the novel, withdrawing affection from her at strategic moments and blaming her for her class position and her blindness to the plight of others; his invented science-fiction tales – published to make him money – recapitulate this class-ridden world, but his perspective cannot clearly see the woman's own entrapment. Iris's escape, therefore, is not into a new narrative of happily ever after, but into another dead end.

Alex's death in the war finally cuts off any hopeful and romantic conclusion. It is at this point that Laura returns, falsely believing that sacrificing her body to Richard would have ensured Alex's safe passage through the war. Iris, fearing that Laura and Alex had been lovers, coldly and cruelly announces that they had been lovers and that he was dead. Her words precipitate Laura's suicide. Yet Laura has one last message for Iris; she reveals, in code, Richard's treatment of her, and Iris finally understands how all of the principal players are connected – they are connected through her refusal to see: 'That was the whole story. Everything was known. It had been there all along, right in front of my very eyes. How could I have been so blind?' (*BA* 500).

The theme of blindness is, unsurprisingly, threaded throughout the novel. In Alex's science-fiction tale, the blind assassin is hired to kill a mute sacrificial virgin, but falls in love with her himself, and tries to rescue her (in Iris's version they survive, but in Alex's, they are eventually killed). Hilde Staels considers Iris the blind assassin, given her role in her sister's suicide (Staels 155); Barbara Dancygier thinks it's Alex for his role in the fire that sets in motion the Chase family downfall (Dancygier 145); and Earl Ingersoll speculates whether it is truth, time, or art that is the blind assassin (Ingersoll 2003, 555). The likely answer is that the blind assassin is each of these, and Iris, too, is a victim here.

Early in the novel, Iris reveals that Laura's favourite letter was L, because it began her name, but 'I never had a favourite letter that began my name – *I is for Iris* – because *I* was everybody's letter' (*BA* 88, italics in original). Iris is everyone's and no one's, and by the end, so is Laura, too. She appears to belong to the public and to scholars who want to delve into her life in order to understand her text; but Atwood ensures that this desire is left unfulfilled, not only because Iris refuses to cooperate, but because even if she had, she'd be offering up a body that was not the author's body in any case. Iris recognizes that '[f]or them I am only an appendage: Laura's odd, extra hand, attached to no body – the hand that passed her on, to the world, to them' (*BA* 287). Her confession of authorship, which comes some time after the reader recognizes the truth, does at least allow her to acknowledge Laura as a ghostly collaborator: 'The real author was neither one of us: a fist is more than the sum of its fingers' (*BA* 513).

Thus, in this novel, which won the coveted Booker Prize, Atwood reveals again her skilful control over narrative and genre, her focus on the fractured lives of women and the pain they both endure and pass on to others, and her knowing response to both celebrity and scholarship. Iris closes the novel with these words: 'But I leave myself in your hands. What choice do I have? By the time you read this last page, that – if anywhere – is the only place I'll be' (*BA* 521).

In *Oryx and Crake* (2003), Atwood returns to speculative fiction and creates another dystopia, focusing on one lone survivor of an apocalyptic plague: Jimmy, who renames himself Snowman after the Abominable Snowman. He is, apparently, the only human being left, and he is charged with the survival of the Crakers, a genetically modified people who have been specifically developed to replace humans, but as gentler people with built-in protection against predators, theology and the arts. As the novel progresses, the reader understands that each of these threats – for so they are identified by Crake, the mad scientist who created them (and who is Jimmy's former friend) – is not easily overcome; the urge to understand one's beginnings, and to formulate images of one's creator, cannot, it seems, be genetically wiped away. Jimmy finds himself weaving a mythology of sorts for the post-human individuals and in which he is 'a secondary player', a 'back up demiurge' who will be 'falsely remembered' and unmourned (*OC* 224). There is no one left but him to record the past, which he does, in fits and starts, showing how his own individual past is part of a larger narrative of destruction, and ruing his own blindness – a familiar motif in Atwood's novels.

The environmental concerns Atwood raised in *The Handmaid's Tale* are writ large in *Oryx and Crake*, though instead of theocracy as the dystopian future, she creates a world that valorizes science and lets scientists play God. Atwood moves the reader between the present post-apocalypse and the past, exploring how Jimmy and his friend Crake come to live the lives they do. In specially made, sealed compounds for the rich and privileged, scientists pursue genetic engineering, eternal youth and replaceable body parts whilst those outside the compounds become their guinea pigs and must live with the results of global warming, species annihilation and disease. The scientists create pigoons, animals used to harvest spare organs; rakunks, cute pets made from combining a skunk and a raccoon; and several animals that are disasters and need to be exterminated. The thrill is in the possibility: 'create-an-animal was so much fun, said the guys doing it; it made you feel like god' (*OC* 51). The moral results of such experimentation are apparently never explored – or only explored by those whose fates become dark and twisted; Jimmy's mother first turns her back on science and then abandons Jimmy and the compound, becoming a mirage for Jimmy (though in some senses she always was one) and Crake's father is killed for his thorough knowledge of the company's nefarious plans. Jimmy's memories of his mother are infused with anxiety. He clings onto moments when she appears to be happy: 'She was friendly then, too. She was like a real mother and he was like a real child. But those moods of hers didn't last long' (*OC* 30). The 'realness' of her mother's happiness is in doubt, but Jimmy, who consistently confuses reality and construction, wants the picture-book version of a mother.

His father, similarly, is a man who appears to pretend to be a father: he had a 'hearty way of talking' as if he were 'auditioning for the role of Dad, but without much hope' (*OC* 52). At best, he speaks in clichés; he is not a word man, but a scientist. After Jimmy's mother deserts the family (and is quickly replaced by another woman scientist, Ramona), Jimmy becomes a lonely adolescent, looking for connections with others but finding it only with Crake, an odd and brilliant boy with whom he plays computer games and surfs the net, watching disturbing scenes; and through humour and word craft, as well as, later, with a string of women, none of whom is very real to Jimmy.

The games he plays with Crake include Three-dimensional Waco, Barbarian Stomp, Kwiktime Osama as well as Extinctathon (*OC* 40), a game that Crake never abandons, becoming a Grandmaster through identifying extinct animals. It is, in fact, through this game that Crake adopts his name. He was originally called Glenn, but this is only noted once, and even when they are children, he is referred to as Crake. Jimmy's codename was Thickney, 'after a defunct Australian double-jointed bird that used to hang around in cemeteries' (*OC* 81), but the nickname does not stick. If Jimmy is not exactly thick, he is not considered bright enough in a world that elevates science and scientific brains above art. In another game, Blood and Roses, the achievements of humans – roses – are set against their atrocities, and a roll of the dice determines what happens next: 'If it was a Blood item, the Rose player had a chance to stop the atrocity from happening, but he had to put up a Rose item in exchange' (*OC* 79), with the result that not only was it foreordained that the Blood character would win, but also that 'winning meant you inherited a wasteland. This was the point of the game, said Crake, when Jimmy complained' (*OC* 80).

Jimmy's role throughout the novel is to side with artistic achievements, to see the importance of words and thoughts; to hold onto the past in some form. Crake, on the other hand, is about the future, though Jimmy could not – or did not – foretell just what future it was, despite the fact that Crake revelled in the games of destruction: ' "All it takes," said Crake, "is the elimination of one generation. One generation of anything … Break the link in time between one generation and the next, and it's game over forever" ' (*OC* 223, ellipses mine).

When the boys are surfing the Web, they look at sites related to executions or crimes, pornography or political unrest. The news is done in the nude, as if this is normal; sites relating to suicide are openly displayed, and pornography and executions are viewed side by side, so that 'if you switched back and forth fast, it all came to look like the same event' (*OC* 86). Atwood's dystopic warnings about the destructive nature of the Web, its potential for disseminating what is evil rather than what is good and the subsequent effects on youth, are clear.

It is on a pornography site that the boys first come across Oryx, or someone like her: an eight-year-old sex worker on HottTotts. 'Her name wasn't Oryx, she didn't have a name. She was just another little girl on a porno site' (*OC* 90). Later she is given a name, SuSu (*OC* 129), but again, this is not her real name, and she is never given a firm age, either. In fact, there has to be at least a modicum of doubt that the Oryx they see as a child is the same as the woman they work with as an adult, though both Crake and Jimmy do connect them (despite her protests) and both fall in love with her; and the adult Oryx is also a sex worker (or was, before she was employed to teach the Crakers).

In the original viewing of the girl, Jimmy notes the artifice of the scene, where there is a giggle track playing but the girls themselves look frightened. As in all of the text, what is real and not real are blurred: 'There were at least three layers of contradictory make-believe, one on top of the other. *I want to, I want not to, I want to*' (*OC* 90, italics in original). For whatever reason, the girl moves Jimmy in ways that the others do not: 'Then she looked over her shoulder and right into the eyes of the viewer – right into Jimmy's eyes, into the secret person inside him. *I see you*, that look said. *I see you watching. I know you. I know what you want*' (*OC* 91). If this is true, it is more than Jimmy knows, for he is forever unable to understand his own desires.

By the present tense of the novel, when Oryx is already dead, Jimmy considers how little he really knows: 'Was there only one Oryx, or was she legion? But any would do, thinks Snowman as the rain runs down his face. They are all time present, because they are all with me now' (*OC* 308). As an adult, he wants her to be angry about her childhood, and says he doesn't 'buy' her story. Oryx's reply is intriguing: ' "If you don't want to buy that, Jimmy," said Oryx, looking at him tenderly, "what is it that you would like to buy instead?" ' (*OC* 142). Oryx sees herself as a commodity and works hard to keep his image of her alive, though also a second, slippery image, too – in this she is like Grace of *Alias Grace*, offering up a version of herself for consumption, to satisfy Jimmy's desire, even if that version is one where she is degraded. About the man who may (or may not) have imprisoned her as a sex slave in a garage, Oryx claims that he was a kind man, though she does so 'in a storytelling voice. Sometimes he suspected her of improvising, just to humour him; sometimes he felt that her entire past – everything she'd told him – was his own invention' (*OC* 316). It is indeed inventions that are at the heart of *Oryx and Crake*, those and a moral vacuum that allows science to extend to its logical conclusion despite the risks involved. Atwood argues that science itself isn't bad; 'the bad thing is making all science completely commercial, and with no watchdogs. That is when you have to get very nervous' (Halliwell in Ingersoll 260–1).

Atwood also claims, 'Every novel begins with a *what if*, and then sets forth its axioms. The *what if* of Oryx and Crake is simply, *What if we continue down the road we're already on? How slippery is the slope? What are our saving graces? Who's got the will to stop us?*' (*CP* 323, italics in original).

Jimmy is an odd choice for a sole survivor – or perhaps not. A number of questions are suggested by his survival. Does his talent – with words – remain? Or is he a second-class citizen, a mere 'neurotypical' as is suggested by Crake? (*OC* 203). Is it important that it isn't the best and brightest left behind? Is this part of Crake's plan? (After all, Crake makes the Crakers as less intelligent than homo sapiens.) Does his facility with language actually help – in the telling of the old stories, made new? Howells argues that Atwood has 'always been concerned with the ethics as well as the aesthetics of fiction' (Howells 2005, 171) and Jimmy is an ethical monitor, even if, like Offred before him, he did not always protest enough or strongly, and he did not always see what was right in front of his eyes.

Jimmy quips, 'The prospect of his future life stretched out before him like a sentence; not a prison sentence, but a long-winded sentence with a lot of unnecessary subordinate clauses' (*OC* 188). Yet it is also a sentence of another kind; his solitary, precarious existence means that he can envisage no reader of his words, no one to find him on this deserted land. After a trip to get supplies, Jimmy cuts his foot, and the infection that begins to rage through him may have ruined Crake's final plans, for there may be no one left to look over the Crakers until they establish themselves in their new, uncontrolled habitat. Yet just at this point, Jimmy becomes aware of the presence of others, three people who may wish him and the Crakers harm. He needs to decide – does he run away, engage them or destroy them? The final lines of the novel do not make this clear: 'Zero hour, Snowman thinks. Time to go' (*OC* 374). While Bouson delights in the indeterminacy of the ending, Shuli Barzilai argues that Jimmy/Snowman will side with Crake in keeping the Crakers alive and thus attempt to kill the remaining humans; Danette DiMarco suggests that Jimmy's loneliness will prompt him to risk connection once more if only to satisfy his sexual longings (DiMarco 193), and Howells argues that the choice is not about Crake, but about the women in Jimmy's life: his mother, who wanted him to help her destroy the products of science gone mad, and Oryx, who had elicited a promise from him to protect the Crakers (Howells 2005, 183). After all, Jimmy had said, '"Okay then. Cross my heart and hope to die. Happy now?" It didn't cost him anything, it was all purely theoretical' (*OC* 322).

If the novel is 'purely theoretical', it is based on present-day practices and the potential of scientists to deny the ethics of their acts. Atwood casts an artist's eye over this power, and asks us, the readers, to do the same.

It is clear that Atwood wasn't finished with the story and returned to the environment of *Oryx and Crake* in her next novel, *The Year of the Flood* (2009), which focuses on members of the God's Gardeners cult; Jimmy, Glenn/Crake and Oryx all figure in the novel, and Bernice, Jimmy's roommate in the Martha Graham Academy, is fleshed out more fully, too. Jimmy's erstwhile mother also makes a few appearances, though her flight from the Compounds is shown to be ultimately futile, since the information she passes on to the Gardeners is out of date and useless to them. This is the first time that Atwood has attempted a sequel, of sorts, or perhaps the novel is best identified as companion text, for the action takes place simultaneously with the earlier novel, but from a radically different perspective. Atwood herself has coined the word 'simultaneouel' to describe the novel in interviews to promote the work and there has been some suggestion by one of her publishers, Vintage, that this is the second book in the MaddAddam Trilogy, though other publishers have marketed it as a stand-alone novel. It is clear that the novel could be read on its own, but it becomes a richer text when paired with *Oryx and Crake*.

Atwood returns to the more familiar perspective of female characters, with two women as central focalizers: Toby (also known as Tobiatha) who speaks in the third person and Ren (also known as Brenda), who speaks in the first person. The novel is divided into sections, all prefaced by sermons from Adam One, the leader of God's Gardeners, and an oral hymn, before the reader encounters the present-day Toby or Ren, who delves into the past to connect the experiences of now with the Saint Day of the past. Apart from the very first, the sections are devoted to Toby or Ren respectively, but once the narrative closes in on the present, from Year Twenty-four, the sections start to go back and forth. The very final section takes Ren's perspective alone.

If Jimmy is a compound kid in a gated community, Ren has spent time in the Pleeblands (though ensconced in the Gardener's world, which sees the Pleeblands and everywhere else as the Exfernal world), and her friend Amanda is familiar with the Pleebrats (or the underclass) and is figured as a Texan refugee. Both Ren and Amanda make brief appearances in the earlier novel, as Jimmy's sexual conquests, and Ren has continued to view Jimmy as her first and only true love. Thus, Jimmy is both central and peripheral to the novel as a whole. Amanda's past and her former identity as Barb Johnson is reworked in *The Year of the Flood*; in the earlier novel she claims to be a white-trash refugee; in *The Year of the Flood* she is figured as an orphan. In both, however, her adult life is as a BioArtist, where she uses decay and death aesthetically – as, of course, Atwood herself appears to do.

What Amanda and Ren (amongst others, including Toby) share in common are dysfunctional, dead or absent parents and the cult of God's Gardeners. Like many cults, then, the Gardeners take in refugees, offer a sense of another way of living and rename their members: people of power in the cult become Adams and Eves, with numbers attached to their names to indicate their function (though not their rank, except for Adam One).

Ren is brought into the cult at age seven, by her mother, who runs away from her Compound scientist husband to have an affair with Zeb, one of the Adams; Zeb was a former compound man himself, and he straddles the worlds neatly, donning costumes to blend into the Pleeblands and taking a more aggressive approach than Adam One, the leader of the group. Eventually, Zeb forms a breakaway group, MaddAddam, bioterrorists who also featured in *Oryx and Crake*.

Toby's entry to the cult is more accidental. She is rescued from her job as a meat barista in SecretBurgers (and unwilling sexual hostage of her boss Blanco) by the Gardeners, following a plea from a former colleague Rebecca, and she spends a considerable number of years with the cult, rising to the position of an Eve, despite her lack of faith. ' "In some religions, faith precedes action," said Adam One. "In ours, action precedes faith. You've been acting as if you believe, dear Toby. *As if* – those words are very important to us. Continue to live according to them, and belief will follow in time" ' (*YF* 168, italics in original). Whether belief actually does follow is unclear, but what is clear is that Toby continues to enact the rituals of the cult and their lessons save her life. She is good with potions, bees and mushrooms, but her past always threatens to catch up with her, and once Blanco discovers her whereabouts, she is forced to flee to a new life. Relocated to an AnooYoo Spa, she manages the accounts and staff and continues to stash away her supplies. Despite not believing the creed of the Gardeners, she does feel that her removal from the cult was an 'expulsion' (*YF* 257) and both she and Ren find it hard to deny the teachings of the cult. Gardeners are vegetarians who have taken Vegivows and who consider the term 'meat-breath' one of the worst expressions one can use about another, and they apologize any time they unthinkingly use a cliché or metaphor that suggests violence to animals, such as killing two birds with one stone, or how many ways there are to skin a cat.

Within the space of the novel itself, it is clear that the religion is being manufactured, and the doctrine itself is being constructed. The novel spans the period of Year Five of the cult (the year that Toby joins the cult – reluctantly, it seems, but as a measure of nowhere else to go) to the present, Year Twenty-Five, the Year of the Flood, the year of the BlyssPluss plague. With their new naming of years, the religion sets its own reality. The reader follows the Gardeners through schisms and internal conflict, through tussles over doctrine, and through expulsion or release. Tony, the insider-outsider figure, offers commentary on the work of the Gardeners, not only on their claim that God has an 'aesthetic preference' for long hair on women but also on their 'bossy sanctimoniousness' and the fact that 'the prayers were tedious, the theology scrambled' (*YF* 46). The Gardeners eschew washing and fine clothes; Ren's interpretation of this as a child is '[w]e looked down on these others because their clothes were nicer than ours' (*YF* 141). They avoid writing things down, to avoid capture, and rely on 'instructive rhymes' (*YF* 19) and old medicine: honey as antibiotics; maggots for infection; willow as an analgesic.

They call their storehouses Ararats, presumably after Mount Ararat, where Noah's Ark was said to have come to rest. Since God promised in the Bible never again to send a flood to destroy the earth and its inhabitants, the Gardeners speak of a Waterless Flood. Like many cults, the Gardeners believe that they are the chosen people, and will be saved – they 'exempted themselves' from the predicted disaster (*YF* 47). Although it is seemingly coincidental that so many Gardeners would be saved, it is also perhaps a comment on their preparedness as well as their sense of salvation. Despite their professed vegetarianism and pacificism, the Gardeners are also pragmatic; thus, they require the children to eat meat in their lesson 'Predator-Prey Relationship' and offer 'Urban Blood-shed Limitation' classes, where the lesson is, 'the first bloodshed to be limited should be your own' (*YF* 22).

Adam One, the leader of the group, is a mysterious figure who appears to know exactly what is going on and who spouts doctrine but also banalities. He is also given a sort of mythical power by the children: 'He always seemed to know if there was something unusual going on … it was just like he had a phone' (*YF* 151), which of course he probably does, since he certainly has a computer, despite professing the evilness of the device. This question of having a phone is never answered, but shows up the hypocrisy of the cult, or at least its pragmatism; it also offers a sort of echo back to *Alias Grace*, where Simon purports to uphold the myth of the innate refinement of women because it may 'safeguard the purity of those still pure. In such a cause, hypoc-risy is surely justified: one must present what ought to be true as if it really was' (*AG* 87). Similarly, the Adams and Eves present what ought to be true – no reliance on technology or conventional medicine – as what is true to their followers.

Only Zeb openly flouts the rules of the cult, taking showers every day and disappearing on errands that are never fully disclosed, but which often include violence. Of the Gardeners who survive the Waterless Flood, many of them do not consider themselves real Gardeners; Ren talks about the 'real' Gardener children, Shackie, Croze and Oates, who had been born into the cult or joined it when they were very young (*YF* 59), and she had been forc-ibly removed by her mother when she was in her midteens. In the present tense of the novel, she is working as a sex worker in Scales and Tails, having (like Toby before her) had to quit the Martha Graham Academy before finish-ing her degree. However, the Gardeners' lessons remain with her: '*Beware of words. Be careful what you write. Leave no trails.* This is what the Gardeners taught us, when I was a child among them. They told us to rely on memory, because nothing written down could be relied on' (*YF* 6, italics in original). Amanda had acted as if she had faith, but had merely been 'gleaned' by Ren in Year Ten; that is, she was saved from her Pleebrat fate, though she always keeps at least one part of herself turned to the Exfernal world. Toby her-self has been expelled, in Year Eighteen, 'the year of rupture' (*YF* 240). Thus, they are already outside the cult when the disaster strikes, as indeed are Zeb, Rebecca, Croze, Shackie and Oates, who have all joined MaddAddam instead. The final fate of the firm believers is unclear; they 'go dark' and the last that the reader hears from them is that their numbers have dwindled and many are close to death.

The novel acts a little like a mystery, but one where readers of *Oryx and Crake* know some of the truth, though participants do not; when we are introduced to Glenn/Crake, or Jimmy, or even catch a fleeting glimpse of Oryx, we understand their significance. In other ways, readers of the earlier novel are just as much in the dark as those who have not read it, at first. For example, the reader is confronted with odd images that only become clear later; Toby's hair 'smells of mutton' (*YF* 17), but it is only later that we understand that she has had a Mo'Hair transplant, in order to avoid detection by Blanco. Blanco, a Painball veteran – or one who has managed to survive a prison sentence of enclosure, where two teams fight to the death – is a recurring figure, not only in Toby's world but also in Ren's; he visits the brothel she works in and she is only saved because she has been placed securely in the 'Sticky Zone' as a precaution, where they are checking whether or not she has been infected by one of her clients. It is indeed this precaution that keeps her from illness. Toby is saved because she reads the signs of impending doom and encases herself at the spa after her colleagues have left: 'They had gone home to be with their families, believing love could save them. "You go ahead, I'll lock up," Toby had told them. And she had locked up, but with herself inside' (*YF* 17). The three brothers are saved because they had been locked inside the Painball area just as the plague struck, for their work with bioterrorists. Amanda is saved because she is in the Wisconsin Desert with her art, and she knows enough about survival to avoid people.

Yet not all of those who do survive are good, of course, for Blanco is one such survivor, though, in their final encounter, Toby is the ultimate victor, and she is responsible for speeding up his death, which she rationalizes to herself as inevitable. Blanco's companions are, it appears, the figures who Jimmy witnesses at the end of *Oryx and Crake*, along with their hostage Amanda; so the reader is able to watch from a new perspective that final encounter, where Jimmy raises a spraygun to them but is too weak and confused to shoot in any case. Ren and Toby, working in concert, manage to subdue the men, free Amanda and try to rescue Jimmy, but he is ill, and the reader is given no assurances of his final survival. The novel ends with the motley crew on the beach, and the Crakers singing and about to join them. Thus, it ends only a few hours later than *Oryx and Crake*, but it offers a wider lens and follows the fate of more survivors.

The novel is interspersed with the Gardener's oral hymns, which, in the acknowledgements of the book, Atwood suggests were influenced not only by William Blake and John Bunyan, but also *The Hymn Book of the Anglican Church of Canada and the United Church of Canada*; Atwood also notes, 'Like all hymn collections, those of the Gardeners have moments that may not be fully comprehensible to non-believers' (*YF* 433). The verses have been set to music by Orville Stoeber, thus creating an additional layer to this multi-layered novel, which intersperses the two narratives of Ren and Toby with the voice of Adam One in prayer, and a selection of Saints' Names and Days (with examples such as Saint Stephen Jay Gould, the evolutionary biologist and palaeontologist, and Saint Dian Fossey, celebrated zoologist who was the subject of *Gorillas in the Mist*).

The extra-textual elements of the novel are legion; Atwood also used such foci in *Oryx and Crake*, creating a website www.oryxandcrake.com to go alongside it, pointing readers to historical facts and newspaper clippings, an essay and an interview; Amanda Cole has argued that this is Atwood's way of controlling her narrative 'past what is generally accepted as the perceived limitations, or boundaries, of authorial influence'. However, canny authors have recognized the power of the Web to disseminate information, offer publicity and answer questions (and even market spin-off merchandise). There is a similar website for this novel, www.yearoftheflood.com, where readers can interact with the text; they can provide new Saints' Names (for a small donation), buy merchandise, calculate their carbon footprint and follow Atwood's blog. This is indeed a new arena for the author, and does take the novel outside of its fictional space, especially in its promotion of the fictional God's Gardener's cult. Atwood has argued that 'unless environmentalism becomes a religion it's not going to work' (Wagner 3), so perhaps this is her attempt to create and induce just such a change.

Short stories

Atwood's earliest collection of short stories, *Dancing Girls* (1977), was followed by *Bluebeard's Egg* (1983), *Wilderness Tips* (1991), and the short pieces (including prose-poems) collected in *Murder in the Dark* (1983), *Good Bones* (1992) and *Good Bones and Simple Murders* (2001), an amalgam of the previous two collections. Atwood also published *The Tent*, another collection of fragments or short-short stories (possibly even essays), in 2006, the same year in which her most recent collection of stories, *Moral Disorder*, appeared.[4] Reingard Nischik rightly notes that 'Atwood's commentators have yet to discover an appropriate collective critical term for these varied short texts' (Nischik in Howells 153), which straddle the gap between story, essay and prose poem. With titles such as 'Life Stories,' 'Plots for Exotics' and 'Three Novels I Won't Write Soon', *The Tent* offers up snippets of Atwoodian panache, masquerading as knowledge about the author but as always, slipping back from genuine revelation. In 'Life Stories', the narrator claims: 'I'm working on my own life story. I don't mean putting it together; no, I'm taking it apart. It's mostly a question of editing' (*T* 4) and indeed these pieces are highly condensed, some, like 'No More Photos', extending only to a paragraph. In another piece, 'Encouraging the Young', the narrator claims that this is a new tactic for her, now that she has realized that they are not her rivals: 'Fish are not the rivals of stones' (*T* 17). But it ends on a menacing note: 'I won't fatten them in cages, though. I won't ply them with poisoned fruit items. I won't change them into clockwork images or talking shadows. I won't drain out their life's blood. They can do all those things for themselves' (*T* 19). This is less 'Encouraging the Young' than, in fact, forewarning them of doom and disaster, of the ways in which stories only have one ending, their plots always already written.

In our interview, Atwood confirmed that she writes neither her poetry nor her short stories as collections, but did reveal that 'they accumulate, so that by the time you have maybe five or six of them, you can see the shape that the book is'. Certainly it is the case that within – and between – the collections, there are many links for the careful reader to spot. All of the collections, for example, deal with familiar Atwoodian motifs: nationalism; the politics of power (particularly sexual politics); identities in conflict; the assumption of victimhood. Frank Davey argues that what connects much of Atwood's fiction is the fact that her characters are 'inarticulate about their personal stories, unable to express their fears to one another' (Davey 1986, 10), and that they 'live psychologically in the hidden story while functioning physically in the official story. They dream and think in the language of symbols but they speak in cliché. They trivialize their inner lives in order to live a life of conventional fiction' (Davey 1986, 12–13).

Moreover, the order of individual stories as well as the choice to use a particular story as the title for a collection create meaning for the work as a whole. By the time she published *Wilderness Tips*, Atwood stopped adding the obligatory 'and other stories' phrase to the title, thereby reinforcing the connections between the texts, with the title story acting as a collective title, too. The reader is primed to consider the titular stories as the most significant of the collection, yet their placement – generally near the end of the collections – belies this prominence, and it is not always easy to see why they have been given prominence. Careful reading, however, suggests that the metaphors of the titles work to indicate larger themes in the collections: *Dancing Girls* focuses on younger women who are finding their way in the world, and offers a nod to Atwood's recurrent usage of the Red Shoes story, both in its folk-tale version and in relation to the film starring Moira Shearer. In this collection, the women rarely 'have it all' – they choose, and sometimes poorly, between their options. *Bluebeard's Egg* – a title that connects folk tales and symbols of new beginnings – includes stories where narrative is a central theme, with how a tale is told being as important as what is told (and retold, or rewritten), and *Wilderness Tips* offers an overt reference to Canadian landscape, linking in the images of dominance and submission that have become signature themes for the author.

Davey suggests that, for Atwood, 'the short story always has the iconic potential of poetry – to be oblique and enigmatic, to be a language structure of intrinsic attraction rather than one dependent on the action it narrates' (Davey 1984, 128), and he further argues that the stories grow 'by repetition and accumulation of image and symbol rather than by linear narration' (Davey 1984, 129). Certainly it is the case that Atwood uses and reuses images throughout her oeuvre, and her narrative stance is one often of experimentation, particularly in her short-short stories.

Atwood's first collection of short stories, *Dancing Girls and Other Stories*, brings together fourteen pieces of short fiction, twelve of which had been previously published in the 1970s, on platforms as diverse as *Chatelaine* and *Ms*.[5] The stories are characterized by a sense of miscommunication, or by the sense of an event happening slightly offstage. The heart of several of these stories is an inexplicable departure, a failure to connect events and disappearances, or a lack of communication about the importance of events. In the first of these, 'The Man from Mars', the main character Christine is accosted by a man of uncertain ethnic origin who shadows her, following her around and even coming into her home on one occasion in a parody of a social visit. Christine, who shares her male companions' contempt for other women, finds that the presence of this mysterious man somehow lends her an aura: 'there was something about her that could not be explained. A man was chasing her, a peculiar sort of man, granted, but still a man, and he was without doubt attracted to her, he couldn't leave her alone' (*DG* 24). On the back of this, she is asked out by several men, but no one can understand, exactly, what intrigues her stalker. After he is caught, he becomes an 'amusing story' (*DG* 28), until the point that Christine discovers that she is but one of many women followed by the man. Later, the man is identified as Vietnamese, though only because of the raging war, and just as inexplicably, Christine begins to worry about him. In the final line of the story, in considering his fate, she muses, 'perhaps he had become an interpreter' (*DG* 31). Yet his actions are never fully interpreted or understood; he is a presence who both unsettles and delights Christine, in that his presence reflects back some value onto her, a value she does not obtain intrinsically. The story is left uninterpreted by either Christine or the narrator, and as such, offers a challenge to the reader to discover, again, what it is that makes Christine special.

The second story, 'Betty', focuses upon the summer neighbours of a young girl and her sister; for the girls, Betty's husband Fred is alluring, whilst Betty is not. She is, instead, the proverbial girl next door, the woman who maintained a long-distance relationship with Fred during the War when he was in the Navy. The narrator's childhood voice offers resonances of adulthood, a sense of something not quite understood: 'Betty had written letters to him every single night and mailed them once a week. She did not say how often Fred had written to her' (*DG* 36). The adult narrator understands that their bond of love is unequal; this is eventually made clear to Betty, too, and the couple divorces.

According to the girls' father, Betty was a 'fool', and the narrator notes: 'Later, when husbands and wives leaving each other became more common, he often said this, but no matter which one had left it was always the woman he called the fool. His highest compliment to my mother was that she was no fool' (*DG* 45). Atwood's concise prose offers a clear sense of character – or lack of it. Though it is the woman who is a 'fool' in the father's book, it is clear that he, too, is not what might have been hoped for, for himself, as this passage indicates: 'My father changed jobs again; he was now in building materials, and he was sure, since the country was having a boom, that this was finally the right change' (*DG* 45). The father and Fred are both clearly men who want to be seen to be in charge of their fates, whereas their wives occupy a secondary position.

Later, Betty resurfaces in their lives, becoming important for a while to the girls' mother; then, after an estrangement, Betty dies, leaving the narrator wondering at her own cruelty in being dismissive of the woman: 'I would like her to forgive me for my rejection of her angora mittens, for my secret betrayals of her, for my adolescent contempt. I would like to show her this story I have told about her and ask her if any of it is true' (*DG* 50). In death, Betty becomes what she was not before, despite the title of the story: the focus of attention. The narrator notes that Fred 'no longer intrigues me. The Freds of this world make themselves explicit by what they do and choose. It's the Bettys who are mysterious' (*DG* 50). As in the first story, then, a central female character is offered a reconsideration, a re-evaluation, but in this case, it seems she deserves it.

In 'Polarities', a young American academic, Morrison, is faced by a graduate student, Louise, who is having a breakdown, though at first he is unable to read it as such, partly because he is trying to decide whether or not he is attracted to her. Both colleague and student, Louise is in an in-between situation, and her peculiarities – such as no longer using the telephone – only later become seen in context, as evidence of a slow decline into mental aberration. The switch to a male focalizer works, as he tries to decode her illness: 'Poor Louise, he saw what she had been trying desperately to do: the point of the circle, closed and self-sufficient, was not what it included but what it shut out' (*DG* 74). Although Nischik reads Morrison as disturbed as Louise is, suggesting that he is 'a classic representation of the schizoid personality' (Nischik in Howells 147), this rather overstates the case; he is simply self-absorbed, and unable to reach out fully to Louise or to take her seriously.

Other stories are more clearly about male–female communication break-downs, from the off-centre 'Under Glass' which explores sexual betrayal, to 'The Grave of the Famous Poet' which follows a couple on holiday and the final disintegration of their relationship. At first, the couple seems to be edging towards reconciliation, but this does not last: 'Actually it's less a truce than a rest, those silent black-and-white comedians hitting each other until they fall down, then getting up after a pause to begin again. We love each other, that's true whatever it means, but we aren't good at it; for some it's a talent, for others only an addiction' (*DG* 93). The narrator wants a neat and nice ending, but knows that it will not be so:

> I want it to be over, the long abrasive competition for the role of victim; it used to matter that it should finish right, with grace, but not now. One of us should just get up from the bench, shake hands and leave, I don't care who is last, it would sidestep the recriminations, the totalling up of scores, the reclamation of possessions, your key, my book. But it won't be that way, we'll have to work through it, boring and foreordained though it is.   (*DG* 95)

Here, the sense of repetition, of story, is clear; the couple is not disintegrating, but acting out a script, their parts already known in advance. 'Hair Jewellery' also follows a doomed love affair, but one that, in contrast to the relationship above, never really gets started, though the narrator notes that she is in the process of making up the other lover, and even herself, in looking back; this, she thinks, is 'like conjuring the dead, a dangerous game' (*DG* 101). (In several of her later collections, Atwood returns to the idea of a doomed love affair, or of how the affair becomes, eventually, a story, to be rehashed and rehearsed for different audiences, as she does, for example, in 'The Bog Man' in *Wilderness Tips*.) 'Hair Jewellery' is the story of unrequited love, which, as the narrator notes in retrospect, 'had advantages'. After all, such love 'provided all the emotional jolts of the other kind without any of the risks, it did not interfere with my life, which, though meagre, was mine and predictable, and it involved no decisions' (*DG* 104). Years later, when the couple who weren't quite a couple accidentally meet up at an academic conference, they decide against anything other than a catch-up conversation, both dismayed at the presence of the other, though perhaps for different reasons. The narrator notes: 'I expected you to have been dispelled, exorcised: you had become real, you had a wife and three snapshots, and banality is after all the magic antidote for unrequited love. But it was not enough' (*DG* 118). Instead, he remains a ghost of what might have been, and the narrator cannot quite leave him in the past.

Two of the stories move beyond the smaller canvas of relationships to explore larger political or world issues, though it would be untrue to suggest that the larger world does not matter in the stories focused more on relationships, nor that relationships do not count in the stories which take a wider lens. 'When It Happens' is an apocalyptic tale of impending global disaster and one woman's response to it – she rightly predicts that whatever political takeover is afoot, it will happen quietly, and be censored, so that it will be by silence that she will understand the significance of what has occurred. In some ways, this piece seems to be a forerunner of *The Handmaid's Tale*. Similarly, 'A Travel Piece' concerns a travel writer who is perhaps a prototype of Rennie Wilford in *Bodily Harm*. Annette finds that her travels remain boringly undisturbed because those who greet her are prepared for her presence and ensure that she does not see anything that disturbs her view. Even when the plane she is travelling in crashes, she begins to think that this is not quite a story: 'For a moment she thought something real had happened to her but there is no danger here, it is as safe in this lifeboat as everywhere else, and the piece she would write about it would come out sounding the same as her other pieces' (*DG* 139). Yet this story ends without resolution, as the lifeboat, full of people who may be lying to each other, is still at sea and one member is at risk, either because of his own stupidity or in relation to the malice of others. Annette notes, 'She is a professional tourist, she works at being pleased and at not participating; at sitting still and not watching' (*DG* 143), but these are close quarters, and what happens at the end demands her participation, or at least consent, though she withholds both by ending on the question, 'Am I one of them or not?' (*DG* 143).

In 'The Resplendent Quetzal', which also concerns travel, the first focalizer is Sarah, a bored wife whose bird-loving husband Edward is getting on her nerves. She sends him off on various pursuits, pretending to see a flash of wing that excites him so that she can get peace: 'That was enough to send him off. She had to do this with enough real birds to keep him believing, however' (*DG* 147). They seem in a familiar rut, that of the long married who find each other irritating rather than exciting, but this reading is a false one; the story shifts to

Edward, and the tone darkens, before shifting back to Sarah again. Edward is not the uncomprehending fool Sarah seems to think he is. He is enraged and thinks of Sarah as 'devious' and 'incredibly stupid' (*DG* 147). Yet it is telling that, having known about her ruse for three years, he continues to pretend to believe her when she sends him away. When the story returns to Sarah, it continues to pursue a dark theme, in that she idly imagines his death: 'Sarah was speculating about how she would be doing this whole trip if Edward had conveniently died. It wasn't that she wished him dead, but she couldn't imagine any other way for him to disappear' (*DG* 151). The tension between presence and absence is central to the story, with Edward's presence and absence coexisting: Sarah felt 'deserted' by Edward after the death of their child (*DG* 157), a revelation that comes late in the story. This loss offers an explanation for their estrangement, though it is clear that neither one of them understands this fully. The dead child is a blockage that they cannot get past; inexplicably, Sarah steals a baby Jesus from a crèche scene outside a restaurant. In this very last section, the movement from Sarah to Edward's perspective is not notified by a line break – rather, the story continues, just as Sarah goes near a sacrificial well with the baby Jesus. Edward is afraid she's thinking of jumping in, but finds it even harder to deal with her tears – she has not, he thinks, cried for the lost baby in the past, though this may only be his version of events. For each, the missing child equates with a chasm that cannot be filled, and neither is able to decode the symbols of their estrangement. Thus, this story melds the inner and outer worlds, the impact of travel and tourism and the problematics of a relationship in need of repair that is, instead, being ignored.

In 'Training', a potential medical student spends a summer at a camp for disabled children, making a clear connection with one child, Jordan, despite the fact that she cannot communicate verbally. Significantly, she is the only one who sees his final betrayal, when a performance put on for the entertainment of the group becomes, for him, a perverse and grotesque performance that reveals what the children cannot do, not what they can. His response – unbridled laughter – is a betrayal that she witnesses – but cannot communicate to others, thus rendering him 'safe' (*DG* 182). Ironically, perhaps, this experience prepares him for exactly what he had been resisting: the world of medicine, which treats patients as commodities and not individuals.

The question of betrayal is also evident in the next story, 'Lives of Poets', where Julia performs at poetry readings in order to keep her and her boyfriend solvent, even though she finds the readings damaging and oppressive. She finds that creative-writing students feed off her in ways that are uncomfortable, and she longs to tell them: '*don't make the mistakes I made*. But what was her mistake? Thinking she could save her soul, no doubt. By the word alone'

(*DG* 193, italics in original). This conflation of writing and salvation does not work, however. Near the end of the story, while attempting to call her lover Bernie, she gets his friend Marika instead, and from this (possibly) innocent call, Julia launches into a fear that he is having an affair. The story ends in the future tense – an underused tense in creative writing, which perhaps explains its usage here – but with no clear answers as to whether her intuition is right or very wrong.

'Dancing Girls' comes near the end of the collection, and focuses on a boarding house and its occupants, who are mostly foreign students, thus returning to the earlier theme of intercultural (mis)communication. 'The Sin Eater' focuses on a psychiatrist, Joseph, and the mess he leaves behind after what appears to be an accidental (and absurd) death – falling out of a tree. He also leaves behind two ex-wives and a current wife, as well as a number of female patients who may or may not be in love with him. The final story, 'Giving Birth', metafictionally follows a woman in labour; the narrator, a writer, writes the story of the woman who ends up seeing a doppelgänger pregnant woman who is clearly not pregnant by choice. The writer muses on the language of giving birth: 'How can you be both sender and the receiver at once? Was someone in bondage, is someone made free' (*DG* 225); she also considers giving birth as a 'performance' for the husband of the tale (*DG* 229) who is otherwise left out of the sending and receiving equation. The story – and thus collection – ends with the birth: 'in the days that follow Jeanie herself becomes drifted over with new words, her hair slowly darkens, she ceases to be what she was and is replaced, gradually, by someone else' (*DG* 240).

In *Bluebeard's Egg*, the reader sees a developing Atwood. This collection, though certainly still dealing intensely with breakdowns in communication between men and women – or the kinds of adjustment that men and women make to try to stay together or live apart successfully – is also much more infused with the stories of generations – with parents taking up significant space in both the first story and those nearing the end, where ageing also takes on some resonance. The twelve stories, of which 'Bluebeard's Egg' comes sixth, contain a variety of contact points: myths and folk tales; strong but silent women; and relationships that are doomed by miscommunication, deliberate or otherwise. The process of storytelling, or narrating, is key to each of the stories. 'Significant Moments in the Life of My Mother', for example, explores the stories told by a mother to her daughter, and the daughter's attempt to understand their significance. The adult daughter has to remind herself that these stories are not the culmination of her mother's life, but merely 'punctuation' (*BE* 16). Interpretation of these stories is multiple. A story about dead baby chicks, pets of the mother's childhood, for example, gets this gloss: 'Possibly this story is meant by my mother to illustrate her own stupidity, and also her sentimentality … Possibly it's a commentary on the nature of love; though knowing my mother, this is unlikely' (*BE* 11). Yet it is this very knowingness that comes under question, under threat, and it is also clear that stories have specific listeners: some are meant only for women, and some are meant as a way of tightening the familial bond. Barbara Godard suggests that the audience is complicit in the tales which suggest that the family itself had only narrowly avoided disaster and death (Godard 76). Certainly, the narrator notes: 'When she is in a certain mood, we are to understand that our lives have been preserved only by a series of amazing coincidences and strokes of luck; otherwise the entire family, individually or collectively, would be dead as doornails' (*BE* 22). The use of colloquial phrases is not accidental; it is the voice of the storyteller mother coming through the narrator's own.

Indeed, it is strikingly clear that the stories are themselves performances, something that the daughter understands: 'Her eyes gleam, sometimes a little wickedly, for although my mother is sweet and old and a lady, she avoids being a sweet old lady. When people are in danger of mistaking her for one, she flings in something from left field; she refuses to be taken for granted' (*BE* 17). Stories give her power that she would not otherwise obtain: the power to amuse, or inform or impart. Perhaps most significantly, though, the stories are told to gender-specific audiences; any story with blood, betrayal, bodies or diseases is told only to women: 'Men are not to be told anything they might find too painful; the secret depths of human nature, the sordid physicalities, might overwhelm or damage them' (*BE* 22). In a reversal of the usual divisions, here it is women who are considered strong, and men who are believed to be weak and in need of protection. Yet the narrator sees another story behind the story that is told: 'Men, for some mysterious reason, find life more difficult than women do. (My mother believes this, despite the female bodies, trapped, diseased, disappearing, or abandoned, that litter her stories.)' (*BE* 22). The narrator, it seems, knows better, but in fact, both perspectives can coexist. Charlotte Sturgess argues that in Atwood's shorter fiction,

> Just as clichés of femininity and masculinity are constantly foregrounded, so the very concentrated 'self'-centered (rather than plot-centered) forms of short fiction allow for condensations, plurality of genre, multiplicity of perspective. They favor the collapsing of fixed categories that are a central issue in all of Atwood's work.
>
> (Sturgess in Nischik 95)

If the mother becomes powerful through words, this is not always the case for other female characters in the book. In 'Loulou; Or, the Domestic Life of the Language', Loulou is an artist and cook who lives with a variety of men, ex-husbands and ex-lovers – collectively called 'the poets' – who run a collective poetry magazine. She becomes, for them, a muse, or someone onto whom to hang language. She has to look up the words themselves and the story focuses on the power play associated with language. Although the men appear to be cruel to her, mocking her lack of knowledge, they are in fact in thrall to her. Sturgess suggests that Loulou's profession as a potter links her into 'a stereotypical representation of woman as mother earth' but that Atwood turns this story around by offering Loulou 'singular definition and contours for the reader, whereas the poets are designated collectively and are seemingly interchangeable' (Sturgess in Nischik 91). The 'domestic life' is thus far from conventional, and in fact, near the end of the story, Loulou beds an accountant to see if this changes her – if numbers rather than words can offer power.

A collapsing of fixed categories is also apparent in 'Hurricane Hazel', where the narrator knows that she is supposed both to be a good girl and also to react to her boyfriend's continued pressure to have sex; she knows that she is supposed to be a normal girl, but also knows that her family background precludes this; she knows that her summer getaway is supposed to be to a cottage, but knows that it is really a shack. Most importantly, she knows that she does not feel the way she is expected to feel about her boyfriend, but cannot articulate why. Her knowledge only really comes retrospectively, though it is partially presented as if happening also in the present, as in this passage: 'It would not take very much to make Buddy happy, ever: only something like this [lying next to him on his bed]. This was what he was expecting of me, this not very much, and it was a lot more than I had. This was the most afraid I ever got, of Buddy' (*BE* 55). Buddy is not violent, or crazed or in any way abusive; he is a gentle boy who expects the world to fit into his simple version of it, a version with clear gender lines, and the girl knows she cannot, though she also cannot find a way to break it off – until a hurricane comes to Toronto, and she refuses to go out with him. Thus, they break up – the first of many breakups the narrator associates, somewhat anomalously, with weather, as if responsibility for such hurts must lie outside her.

Other stories of relationship dissolutions include 'Uglypuss', in which two activists split up as a result of repeated infidelity, the result of which is a kidnapped cat; and 'Walking on Water' (one of 'Two Stories about Emma') in which a fearless woman falls in love with all the wrong men. The narrator notes: 'Why she can't spot this kind of man a mile off, especially after all that practice, I don't know. But as I've said, she's fearless. The rest of us have more self-protection' (*BE* 122). (The other story about Emma, in fact the first one, is called 'The Whirlpool Rapids', and seeks to explain this fearlessness, suggesting that it is a result of Emma's brush with death when she was 21.) The narrator, who is the same narrator for both stories, suggests that providence protects fearless women, 'maybe out of astonishment' (*BE* 111), but that Emma herself thinks of herself as completely normal. This story is told entirely without dialogue, except for one short exchange in which Emma asks strangers which country she is in, after a Niagara rafting disaster. The answer, 'Canada', is all she needs to know (*BE* 17). This experience, the narrator thinks, has made Emma the fearless – and somewhat feared – individual that she is: 'Because she found out early how little difference she makes in the general scheme of things, she has clenched her teeth, ignored whimpers and hints and even threats, and done what she has wanted, almost always. For this she has been called selfish and unfeeling' (*BE* 118).

By whom she is called such things is not stipulated, though there is more than a suggestion that by taking on such so-called masculine characteristics, Emma has induced apparently feminine characteristics in the men around her. A vital question to ask, therefore, is whether behaviour can ever be seen as anything but gendered. Is she brave and fearless *for a woman*, as the narrator seems to suggest, or brave and fearless, full stop? And what difference might there be? In the same way that Sarah in 'The Resplendent Quetzal' is seen as emotionless (but isn't) because she refuses to mourn publicly for her lost child, so too is Emma judged by those around her for failing to submit to the expected social mores (though at the same time, she is also vaguely admired). That the narrator must attach her to all the wrong men offers an interesting counterpoint; it is as if her fearlessness must be balanced out by something else.

Similarly, in a story near the end of the collection, 'The Sunrise', the main female character becomes a stalker who follows men. She does so for artistic reasons, and most respond well to her advances: 'They've been singled out as unique, told they are not interchangeable. No one knows better than Yvonne how seductive this is' (*BE* 242). Like Loulou, though, Yvonne remains a mystery herself, and her landlords foist different versions of her life onto her.

The disjuncture between what is seen and what may exist is a staple of Atwood's work, and the title story from the collection, 'Bluebeard's Egg', offers a good example of this tendency. Sally is married to, and in love with, Ed, whom she believes to be stupid; there is no evidence for this belief, and indeed evidence to the contrary, given that Ed is a heart surgeon. Sally is his third wife, and as the story progresses, it becomes clear that she, too, might shortly be replaced. At one point, being frustrated that she has not had 'the whole story' of the failure of his first two marriages, Sally muses, 'What if he wakes up one day and decides that she isn't the true bride after all, but the false one? Then she will be put into a barrel stuck full of nails and rolled downhill, endlessly, while he is sitting in yet another bridal bed, drinking champagne' (*BE* 134). In exploring this fantasy, Sally is influenced by the latest night class she is taking, 'Forms of Narrative Fiction', and particularly by the oral tale of Bluebeard, which is, perhaps paradoxically, *written into* the short story (or, at least a version of it). In this way, Atwood metafictionally recycles the Bluebeard tale. Importantly, for her rewriting of it, Sally cannot decide which viewpoint to take; she thinks most roles are too obvious but then when she lights on the idea of the perspective of the egg, is stumped with how to go about it and it is only as she discovers that Ed has affection for another that the reader sees the story being rewritten again. Significantly, however, Sally's own story, her inner life, which the teacher had urged her to explore, remains unwritten at the end.

The rest of the stories in the collection focus on families which have had disease, disruption or divorce. 'Spring Songs of the Frogs' centres on Will, who is trying and failing to date, and his discomfiture with his eighteen-year-old niece, who suffers from an eating disorder; 'Scarlet Ibis' features an unhappily married couple on holiday with their four-year-old daughter. A day trip to a swamp to see birds almost ends in disaster when their tourist boat springs a leak, but in Chaucerian fashion, a Mennonite woman plugs the hole with her bottom, thus allowing the visit to go ahead. In 'The Salt Garden', a single mother, Alma, begins to have hallucinations, or perhaps seizures. Her estranged husband Mort thinks that they are brought on by stress, whereas her lover thinks that they're the result of his sexual prowess; what joins the two men is that 'they've both elected themselves as the cause of these little manifestations of hers' (*BE* 208). In 'In Search of the Rattlesnake Plantain', the narrator's ill father has a stroke, and looks for things that are disappearing, in a clear concern over ageing and imminent death. The final story of the collection, 'Unearthing Suite', again focuses on ageing parents. In recounting her parents' various habitations, the narrator notes: 'Not all of these things are in the same place at the same time: this is a collective memory' (*BE* 268). Moreover, she notes, 'As a child I wrote small books which I began with the words *The End*. I needed to know the end was guaranteed' (*BE* 270, italics in original). That this is the last story of the collection – the end – is not accidental.

Atwood's next significant collection, *Wilderness Tips*, collects together ten stories, many of which have an environmental theme or a focus on landscape. There is a clear evocation of childhood in these stories, as well as decades such as the 1960s. In common with the other collections, there is a focus on lost love, as well as an increasing sense of narrativization. The opening story, 'True Trash', for example, focuses on resisting readers – readers who know the story and plot that they are supposed to find pleasurable or fulfilling, but who read against the grain of the stories' narratives. 'True Trash' is the nickname given to the *True Romance* stories that the young waitresses read during their time off from looking after rich young boys at an exclusive summer camp.

The young women are resistant readers of the magazine and its messages of temptation, betrayal and repentance. They see the heroines of the stories as weak and foolish, too easily led to tears. When one young protagonist sees her potential lover like an '"*animal stalking its prey*"' (*WT* 6, italics in original), the women name the animal a '"weasel"' or '"skunk"' (*WT* 6). When the girl of one of the stories says her body is crying out for his, they ask what it says, and another replies, '"Hey, body, over here!"' (*WT* 7).

These interjections are only sometimes assigned to individual women, but silent throughout is Ronette, who offers only 'an off-centre smile, puzzled, a little apologetic' (*WT* 7) and who asks, '"why is it funny?"' It is, for Ronette, too much like real life, and it is no coincidence that she is the one who ends up getting 'caught' in the end, her narrative ending assured by the ripeness of her body and her ease in offering it up, offering it away. 'True Trash' is also, of course, a name given to the women themselves, particularly Ronette, who has a reputation for being easy. 'Cheap' is another name for them, though this, too, gets redefined by one of the campers, Donny: 'It's an enticing word. Most of the things in his life are expensive, and not very interesting' (*WT* 2).

Whilst the women are reading, they are also being read – or their bodies are. The boys of the camp take turns in viewing them through binoculars, acting out lust that they may or may not really feel. The waitresses, who know they are being watched, taunt the boys a little, 'causing Ritchie, who now has the binoculars, to groan in a way that is supposed to madden the other boys, and does' (*WT* 3). The boys read the signals they are supposed to, and react accordingly, though Donny admits, only to himself, that he would 'like to know what they're reading with such absorption, such relish, but it would be dangerous for him to admit it. It's their bodies that count. Who cares what they read?' (*WT* 3). The tension between reading and being read is sustained throughout. One of the waitresses, Joanne, views Ronette as possessing secret knowledge, but also knows that she herself has 'a bad habit of novelizing' (*WT* 13) and thus, that this assigned secret knowledge may not exist. As a matter of fact, Ronette ends up pregnant at the end of the summer, thereby fulfilling her narrative role as fallen woman, but this time, pregnant by a boy, thereby disrupting the narrative. Joanne, who only latterly discovers this secret, wonders at the end, when meeting the grown-up Donnny: 'Should she tell him? The melodrama tempts her, the idea of a revelation, a sensation, a neat ending' (*WT* 33). But such an ending would not be neat, and therefore Atwood leaves the reader in suspension, with Joanne deciding not to tell and the main male character remaining unaware of his place in the narrative trajectory of the women.

The neatness of an ending eludes many in the collection; Kat, a fashion art-ist who discovers that both her job and her man are off limits to her after an operation to remove an ovarian cyst, wraps up the hairy tumour as a present to her lover and his wife, feeling both feverish and somehow justified, but also 'temporarily without a name' (*WT* 52) at the end of the story 'Hairball'. There is no one word for someone who so publicly outs her relationship after it has ended, and she has already stripped her name down from Katherine via Kathy to Kat. There is nowhere else to go.

Similarly, for Richard, in 'Isis in Darkness', the ending he hopes for resists him. Wanting to become a poet, but settling instead for becoming an academic, he falls in love with Selena, a female poet who gains some limited success in life, but more in death. They meet infrequently, often at the turning of the decade, but their meetings are never satisfying to him. Selena dies somewhat tragi-cally, as befits a doomed female artist, and is resurrected in unlikely fashion by Richard. Having craved transformation through her, in a sense he achieves this by 'summoning up whatever is left of his knowledge and skill, kneeling beside her in the darkness, fitting her broken pieces back together' (*WT* 81). It is sig-nificant that this lost feminist poet is put back together by a man, but it is also significant that this resurrection is one that reflects more on him than on her, as his gloss on their relationship indicates: 'He will exist for her at last, he will be created by her, he will have a place in her mythology after all' (*WT* 80).

If Richard creates Selena, Julie recreates her lover Connor in 'The Bog Man'. After claiming, '*I broke up with Connor in the middle of a swamp*' (*WT* 82, italics in original), Julie retells the tale of a love affair with her professor, with whom she travels to Scotland as a sort of assistant, a ruse that fools nobody. Set in the early 1960s, Julie claims that when the affair took place, 'There was no such phrase as "sexual harassment," even. There was no such thought' (*WT* 84); whether this is seen as a positive or negative thing is left hanging. Certainly, the reader finds that the affair, when it sours (after Julie unexpectedly asks if he'll marry her), has a negative effect on all parties – though surprisingly more on Connor than Julie. When he returns, months later, he seems broken, and follows her from her new apartment, eventually trapping her in a phone box. He leaves only after she calls the police, because, as she notes, 'Whatever else he wanted, he did not want to be caught in the act of sexually attacking a phone booth. Or this is how Julie puts it, when she tells the story these days' (*WT* 102).

In telling this story, Julie takes artistic licence, revising everything includ-ing the principal players, though 'Connor's wife stays approximately the same, but she was an invention of Julie's in the first place, since Julie never met her' (*WT* 82). There are things she does not include, such as grief, or damage – to either party. The story becomes, she realizes, 'a story about her own stupidity, or call it innocence, which shines at this distance with a soft and mellowing light' (*WT* 104).

As these stories make clear, it is only with the benefit of distance that these relationships can be seen differently, though there is no guarantee that this distance makes anything clearer. It can, in fact, obscure or reform the truth of the moment, so that it becomes something else entirely. Certainly, this is the case with 'Death by Landscape', which, like 'True Trash', is set in a summer camp, and in which the main character, Lois, sees things with at least two lenses – that of the present, in which she is a widow, living alone, and of the past, when she was a girl in thrall to another girl, an American named Lucy. For Lois, Lucy represents the foreign and familiar in one; she is from the USA, 'where the comic books came from, and the movies' (*WT* 111), but her mother had been Canadian at one time, and they both experience a raiding of native culture by the camp's director, who likes to pretend that they are native scouts off on adventures. One such adventure has deadly consequences as Lucy disappears and Lois is seen as a potential culprit, rather than a victim herself. The Canadianness of the setting is highlighted here, and recreated by Lois in adulthood, when she spends vast sums on landscape paintings, searching for her lost friend, and never finding her there. Resonances of Atwood's poem 'This is a Photograph of Me' are unmistakable, for, as Lois reveals, 'Every one of them is a picture of Lucy' (*WT* 128).

The collection concludes with stories about relationships in disarray. 'Uncles' follows a successful woman writer who is surprised and dismayed by her male mentor's eventual betrayal of her; her careful femininity is under threat by this betrayal, as she re-evaluates her past appreciation by men, including her uncles: 'Loss of face, the Japanese called it. They knew. She felt as though her face, so carefully prepared and nourished, had been ripped off' (*WT* 156). Thus Atwood returns to questions of femininity and power, and the myriad ways of undermining women. 'Hack Wednesday' also revolves around a woman writer, and her relationships with her husband and co-workers over the period of a day in which both nothing happens and the world seems to shift: 'What happens to this day? It goes where other days have gone, and will go' (*WT* 248). 'The Age of Lead' contrasts the Franklin expedition, where the group died of lead poisoning, with a contemporary unnamed plague, presumably AIDS, which is similarly unfathomable. In 'Weight', a former female lawyer works for a charity for battered women, in remembrance of her friend Molly, also a lawyer, with whom she played word games: 'Here's one for you, Molly. *Menopause*. A pause while you reconsider men' (*WT* 183, italics in original). This pause is, however, a poignant one, for Molly had been killed by her partner, and the lawyer is herself almost prostituting herself to raise money to protect other women from such violent men. The title story focuses on George, an immigrant, and his wife Portia, who is the youngest of three daughters, all of whom have been involved with George; Portia must decide to ignore his infidelities in order to maintain balance, but it is clear that this decision, though practical, marks a significant departure from Atwood's other depictions of infidelity, where such behaviour generally signifies dissolution of relationships, rather than an uneasy maintenance of them.

Unlike her previous work, *Moral Disorder* offers a set of mostly realistic pieces that detail aspects of Atwood's own biography, in a change from her earlier work which disavowed overt connections with her own life. This final collection is, as the Bloomsbury hardback dust jacket notes, 'a collection of eleven stories that is almost a novel … or a novel broken up into eleven stories'. Perhaps the best definition of the book is as a short-story cycle. Although Atwood's earlier collections work as entities in themselves, they are not constructed as such, whereas the component parts of *Moral Disorder* offer a clear link, as well as a semiautobiographical narrative tracing house moves, ghostly visitors, photograph albums, ageing parents and ageing bodies, as well as characters who recur. Nell and Tig are the focal points, and sometimes appear in the first person, and at other times in the third. The first story, 'Bad News', offers a fanciful moment of retreat from present-day anxieties, only to discover that the past holds worse terrors, but the other stories delve into more recent personal history. 'The Art of Cooking and Serving' includes a meditation on the appearance of maids, an image that is used on the front cover of the book itself. In this story, the young protagonist finds her life turned upside down by the arrival of a new baby in the house, as well as her own impending adolescence; the confluence of these events leads her to imagine 'another, more secret life spread out before me, unrolling like dark fabric' (*MD* 26). 'The Headless Horseman' continues the story of the struggle between sisters, and the slow realization that the younger sibling has problems that an older sister cannot name or solve. Here, there are resonances of *The Blind Assassin*, though without the tragic outcome (despite the fact that fear drives the older sister to keep the relationship intact as much as possible). 'My Last Duchess' refers to Browning's poem of the same name, being taught to high-school students by a favoured English teacher, and the links between the poem and the narrator's life. The girl has had a series of boyfriends: 'The process of replacement was delicate – it called for diplomacy, and nuance, and the willpower to resist answering the phone – but at a certain stage it had to be done' (*MD* 69), yet the girl does not fully recognize the link. The lessons she learns in English class seem to be less the lessons that the teacher expects her to memorize than the earlier lessons also taught to the women in 'True Trash': that female characters are wimps. She appears to refuse to bend to the fate of others, but cannot understand why her teacher makes her read the classics. She decides that her teacher had knowledge to impart that was 'hidden within the stories' (*MD* 85), and it was her job to decode it for herself – a metafictional nod to the question of authorship and readership.

This story is followed by 'The Other Place', which explores the narrator's early life on her own, and her attempts to find out more about herself and her art. The narrator recalls, 'That was all quite long ago. I see it in retrospect, indulgently, from the point I've reached now. But how else could I see it? We can't really travel to the past, no matter how we try. If we do, it's as tourists' (*MD* 100). It ends, however, in the present, with a dream that unsettles the narrator, who cannot be comforted. 'Monopoly', set in the early 1970s, turns to the third person and the delicate problem of adultery, and here Atwood again plays with the idea of story: the story of whether or not Nell and Tig would achieve a lasting relationship, given that Tig continues to be married at the point at which they decide to move to the country. It also explores language and game-playing. The narrator feels bewildered by a changing world in which the old rules no longer exist; in her previous life, she had felt that her relationships 'had plots' (*MD* 120), and the idea of infidelity was unthinkable. This collection of stories revisits the emotional geography of *Life Before Man*, with a young woman interrupting an already faltering marriage. Nell feels as if she were manipulated into this position by the wife, Oona, and is seen as little more than a governess – hence her hesitation at finally committing to the farm and to Tig, though by the end of this story, Nell has agreed to stay.

In the title story, 'Moral Disorder', the couple buy a farm. That they are fundamentally unprepared for the reality of living in the country is also a comment on their preparedness for their own relationship. Nell tries to locate her position within a moral framework (after all, Tig is still married), but acknowledges that she could find 'no word for herself that would be both truthful and acceptable' (*MD* 135). The story recounts Tig's enthusiasms for livestock and Nell's for gardening, neither of which results in much success, as animals run away, get injured or die and as plants wither or overproduce. In one instance, pigs from a neighbouring farm actually breach their fences rather than the other way around, and Nell concedes, 'A boundary was only a boundary if you could defend it' (*MD* 149), a comment as much on her relationship with Tig as it is about the land.

The next story, 'White Horse', draws together seemingly unconnected things: Nell's pregnancy; the arrival of a horse, which Nell goes from dreading to loving, and which is finally killed in an accident; her relationship with her mother, which is strained by Nell's unconventional lifestyle (Nell had hoped that the horse might tempt her mother to visit); and the arrival at the farm of her sister Lizzie, who first acts as a go-between for Nell and her parents, and is later diagnosed – wrongly – as a schizophrenic. It is also the first mention of haunting, yet what is clear is that the story itself deals with haunting in several forms: the way in which the presence of domesticity and conventionality haunts the narrator, who desires respectability and security; the way in which Ooona haunts Nell as a superior and original spouse; the way in which the animals themselves cannot survive the disasters of the farm. The final image is of Nell attempting to take on a new role, of seeing herself as a wise woman who knows how to deal with the catastrophes of the farm and of life.

The following story, 'Entities', moves the couple back to the city, and to a series of houses, all bought and sold with the help of Lillie, a concentration-camp survivor who unravels as the story progresses, descending into Alzheimer's. Similarly, Oona herself weakens, though her hold on Nell remains until her death from a stroke – in a house that Nell had bought for her. Nell is persuaded by Lillie to try a form of exorcism, but the 'entities' that apparently inhabit the house are simply seen as an entertaining story by the new inhabitants. Nell muses, 'All that anxiety and anger, those dubious good intentions, those tangled lives, that blood. I can tell about it or I can bury it. In the end, we'll all become stories. Or else we'll become entities. Maybe it's the same thing' (*MD* 213). Again, Atwood's later work is clear in its focus on the construction of stories, of how life can be made into a narrative (as much of this collection appears autobiographical, such musings come to the fore). Similarly, the penultimate story, 'The Labrador Fiasco', traces the decline of the narrator's father against the adventure story of Hubbard and Wallace, two young Americans who, in 1903, attempt to map the Labrador wilds. They are destined to fail – they take the wrong equipment and do not listen to (or understand) the advice they are given; only Wallace survives, along with their Cree guide, George, and even then, only barely. The story is read to and by the father as he succumbs to a second stroke; they never reach the end of the story, stuck as they are awaiting rescue, and with Nell unable to be the guide that her father wants her to be. The story resembles an earlier story, 'In Search of the Rattlesnake Plantain', where the narrator's father also suffers a stroke and where maps do not prove to be as useful or accurate as first hoped. Like that earlier story, it is told in the first person, as is the last story, which focuses on the narrator's mother. Both stories might be told by Nell, but neither names her; in the final one, 'The Boys at the Lab', Nell is the name of a horse her mother loved. This story reveals the narrator trying to tell her mother's stories back to her, since, elderly and frail, 'she can't carry a plot' by herself (*MD* 238). It is elegiac, and its position – at the end – is not accidental. Atwood explores how stories are constructed, reconstructed and, always, partial.

Poetry

Atwood is the author of fifteen books of poetry, from her earliest collection, *Double Persephone* (1961), which was published privately before she graduated from the University of Toronto, to *The Door* (2007). The title of her first collection suggests some of Atwood's evolving and then recurrent creative concerns: doubling, mirror shapes and, of course, the importance of myths. Gordon Johnston argues that 'the past for her is historical, geological and mythic as well as personal' (Johnston 167) and it certainly is the case that Atwood weaves these disparate elements together in much of her poetry, which sets a sense of individual conflict against a larger canvas. Her most recent compilation, *Eating Fire* (1998), is a selection of her best poems from 1965 to 1995, and for ease and convenience, the majority of my references are to poems that can be found in this one collection, since it spans all of the earlier work.

Given the diversity and scope of Atwood's poetry, it would be reductive to claim that a single theme encapsulates all of them. She does, however, appear to be preoccupied with the problematic relationship between the sexes, a topic that recurs throughout all of her oeuvre. Indeed, some critics suggest that her work is exemplified by violent interactions and miscommunications between the genders. However, such a view implies that her response is always strident. This is not the case, as Atwood's poetry is known as much for her comic, ironic voice as for her highly charged sexual politics. Moreover, it is clear that Atwood does not take the stance that the structures of society are men's fault alone. If a man asserts dominance and a woman asserts helplessness, who is to blame for this state of affairs? As Atwood explores in her critical work *Survival*, adopting the stance of a victim means abdicating responsibility, and this can never be a powerful stance; moreover, both men and women are injured by such divisions.

Primarily a free-verse poet, Atwood carefully balances vision and voice, creating intellectually rich poems ranging from just a few lines ('You Fit into Me') to prose-like poems that number three or four pages in length ('Marrying the Hangman'). Recurring images include reflective elements such as mirrors or water; images of desire; and birth; and recurring motifs include concern with landscape and ecology; a fascination with myth, legends and fairy tales; and objectified women. There is also often a question over who is speaking – and who is listening.

In 'This is a Photograph of Me', from *The Circle Game* (1966), Atwood offers a disturbing perspective, where foreground and background get confused, and time itself is uncertain. The persona addresses an unidentified 'you' and argues that the background of the photograph, which was taken some time in the past, shows a lake, and within the centre of the lake is the speaker: 'The photo-graph was taken / the day after I drowned'. The disembodied voice has no overt gender attached, nor is it clear whether the drowning was an accident, suicide or murder. Peter Klappert suggests that 'everything is overexposed and under-developed' (Klappert 219) in this photograph – and in the poem. The second half of the poem is enclosed in parentheses, effectively suggesting two different images: the calm lake and the dead body. In the closing lines of the poem, the speaker claims, 'if you look long enough, / eventually / you will be able to see me'. Presence and absence are thus set against each other in an unsettling way, and the question of perception is identified but not resolved.

The Animals in that Country (1968) offers an ecological focus and, in the title poem, Atwood suggests that animals in Canada – as opposed to the rest of the world – are simply animals, not representatives of something else, and their deaths are not 'elegant'. The contrast is particularly marked between England, where foxes and hunters enact a traditional dance of sorts, and Spain, where the bull and the bull fighter are figured as matched heroes.

This collection was followed by two that were published in 1970. *The Jour-nals of Susanna Moodie*, in tracing a fictionalized Moodie, remains amongst Atwood's most popular collections. Lothar Hönnighausen suggests that this is because Moodie as a figure offers up 'a congenial female persona for embodying the anxieties and longings of a late twentieth-century woman' (Hönnighausen in Nischik 102), reminding readers that even when texts are placed in the past, they are infused with the concerns of the present. The poems in *Procedures for Underground* have a focus on transformation, meta-morphosis and, again, ecology. Atwood followed this collection with *Power Politics* (1971). Johnston argues that Atwood frequently uses the relationship between men and women as 'the primary means of embodying the opposition or conflict' (Johnston 171), but Atwood is careful to rework familiar oppo-sitions. The first poem from the collection is 'You Fit into Me', a minimalist, almost imagist poem:

> You fit into me
> like a hook in an eye
>
> a fish hook
> an open eye

The importance of the pairing and the order of the words ensure that the reader can never reread the poem in innocence. In this respect, it loosely fol-lows the pattern of William Blake's *Songs of Innocence and Experience*. The first two lines of Atwood's poem refer to a domestic, 'feminine' image: sew-ing. The hook-and-eye pattern is one of the simplest devices there is, which may be why the image has such power. The Amish consider buttons 'proud' and use this clasp for all their clothing, and this emphasis on simplicity (here, deceptive simplicity) is the key to the poem. The image that follows is more 'masculine': fishing. It is also graphically violent, suggesting death and destruction. Thus, in two short stanzas, Atwood is able to imply the interrelationship between feminine and masculine imagery, as well as sexual imagery: 'You fit into me'. The poem is therefore not about the male or the female 'view' or activity, but the relationship between them. Is it a relationship of equals – sewing hook and eye, where one cannot exist (or is at least ineffectual) without the other? Or is it a relationship of unequals – the trapped fish, the aggressive hook? Atwood's poem eludes a definitive interpretation and in this space of indeterminacy, Atwood interrogates her power.

In the mid to late 1970s, Atwood published two new collections, *You Are Happy* (1974) and *Two-Headed Poems* (1978), as well as a compilation entitled *Selected Poems: 1965–1975*. 'Tricks with Mirrors' from the 1974 collection is perhaps amongst the richest and most complicated, with the lover presented as a mirror in ways that recall Virginia Woolf's famous sentiment in 'A Room of One's Own': 'Women have served all these centuries as looking-glasses possessing the magic and delicious power of reflecting the figure of man at twice its natural size' (Woolf 37). In Atwood's poem, mirrors are 'the perfect lovers', reflecting the viewer to him or herself, but Atwood also wants the reader to 'Think about the frame' and explore the other aspects of mirrors; there is a tension in the reflection, as well as a sense of restraint, but one that is challenged: 'Don't assume it is passive / or easy, this clarity / with which I give you yourself'. Maintaining the image requires strength that goes unacknowledged. The mirror desires release, but is faced only with the lover/ reflection standing in front of it, 'combing your hair'. The passive/aggressive binary unsettles the fixed positions that seem to be set up. The 1978 collection includes the title poem 'Two-Headed Poems', which starts with an epigraph relating to the Canadian National Exhibition in 1954, which advertised the presence of Siamese twins as a kind of freak of nature, worthy of viewing. Such an epigraph reminds the reader of historical change, particularly in relation to what is considered acceptable 'entertainment'. The collection also includes paired poems such as 'The Woman Who Could Not Live With Her Faulty Heart' and 'The Woman Who Makes Peace With Her Faulty Heart'. In the first of these heart poems, the persona reveals:

> … most hearts say, I want, I want,
> I want, I want. My heart
> is more duplicitous,
> though no twin as I once thought.

> It says, I want, I don't want, I
> want, and then a pause.
> It forces me to listen

The persona claims that the heart explored here is a real muscle, not an image of saccharine love, and the rhythm of 'I want, I want' appears to mimic the beating of a heart. Yet this recognition of antithesis, and of not knowing what the heart wants, moves it beyond the muscle to something more symbolic, despite the persona's protests. In an interview with Joyce Carol Oates, Atwood claimed: 'For me, every poem has a texture of sound which is at least as important to me as the "argument" ' (Oates in Ingersoll 37) and certainly this poem combines sound and meaning to great effect. *Two-headed Poems* also includes the long prose poem 'Marrying the Hangman', which explores the historical situation in eighteenth-century Quebec whereby a woman could escape hanging through marriage to a hangman, and a guilty man could escape his fate through becoming one. The poem also points to the myth of Orpheus and Eurydice as well as to a specific historical case, interwoven with stories that the female persona is told by her friends, stories of personal damage, of fear, of risk; and indeed the two lovers who escape death perhaps find no more than entrapment of another sort themselves, an image that recurs in Atwood's work, most explicitly in her novel *Alias Grace*, which also deals with a servant who wished to be beautiful and a woman whose fate became tied up with a man who had condemned others.

Atwood follows this collection with two published in the 1980s, *True Stories* (1981) and *Interlunar* (1984), as well as another compilation, *Selected Poems II: Poems Selected and New 1976–1986*. The title poem in *True Stories* teases the reader and withholds information. The persona cautions against wanting a true story, claiming both that she never had it, and that it was lost; the title is therefore parodic: there are no 'true' stories, and no 'stories' at all, but poems that offer stark portraits of women's abuse and pain, which Hönnighausen links to Atwood's growing politicization and work with Amnesty International (Hönnighausen in Nischik 110–11). In 'Torture', the persona details horrific injuries done to a woman, noting that it does not matter which side was responsible: 'such things are done as soon / as there are sides'. The collection includes the long poem 'Notes towards a Poem that can Never be Written' which details further atrocities and which claims that poetry cannot be written about such things – even as the poem itself goes into detail about the necessity of such writing, particularly in countries like Canada where there is no fear of political retribution for telling the truth; the downside is 'you can say what you like / because no one will listen to you anyway'. In 'A Women's Issue', Atwood explores images of sexual abuse and objectification that she revisits in

Bodily Harm. The women (and girls) in the poem are 'exhibits'; what is exhibited are their bodies, enclosed in chastity belts, up for sale in shop windows, mutilated through clitoridectomies (also known as female genital mutilation), raped or forced into prostitution. Here, the 'women's issue' cannot be set aside and forgotten; and Atwood's final line is deeply unsettling: 'Who invented the word *love*?' The unsentimental depiction of abused women's material realities is made even more powerful by this incredulous last line.

Interlunar includes a series of snake poems, of which 'Eating Snake' shows Atwood's preoccupation with the necessity to set the literal and the metaphorical, side by side. The speaker claims to have 'taken the god into my mouth' and deconstructs the phallic imagery, claiming that this snake refers to a real snake, which 'tastes like chicken'. She claims that it was 'mere lunch' and 'only a snake after all'; moreover, she argues that God is 'round'. The references to the Holy Communion take the reader back to the image of taking God into one's mouth as well as the snake's deceit in Christianity; in the Bible, the snake is an evil deceiver who tricked Eve into eating an apple. Thus, Atwood plays on many levels with her imagery, always undercutting the images she sets up with her dry claim, it's just a snake. The collection also includes poems regarding mythic figures, Orpheus, Eurydice, Persephone, as well as The Robber Bridegroom (which was the original title of *Bodily Harm*, and only slightly altered in *The Robber Bride*). Most of these characters are reformulated; Orpheus is seen from behind only, and Eurydice does not want to be rescued. Persephone writes letters to women who fail as mothers, and The Robber Bridegroom wishes he did not have to kill (but nonetheless blames his wives for failing him and refusing to accept him, thus necessitating their deaths). Atwood continues this revisiting of canonical figures in *Morning in the Burned House* (1995), with, for example, 'Helen of Troy Does Counter Dancing' and 'Cressida to Troilus: A Gift' and in her book of prose and poetry, *The Penelopiad* (2005), which retells the myth of Penelope and Odysseus, this time from Penelope's perspective. Atwood does not let any of these mythical characters off the hook; she examines motive and internal justifications for acts that others do not understand.

In 'Helen of Troy Does Counter Dancing', the infamous Helen battles against feminist critics who think she is selling out, as well as against men's beery visions of her as provoking either hatred or 'bleary / hopeless love'. She justifies her profession by suggesting that everyone is exploited, and she is simply choosing the easiest way with the most financial reward. But underlying this casual stance is a canny woman who exploits those who try to exploit her. She singles out one spectator as different, as special, knowing that by doing so, she'll entrap him: 'Not that anyone here / but you would understand'. It is the reader who sees beyond bravado and recognizes why the poem also contains images of garbage, death and rape, 'bleak exhaustion' and revenge. Helen claims, 'nothing is more opaque / than absolute transparency'. She offers up an image of transparency precisely to withhold that which appears to be offered: herself.

Atwood's penchant for recycling images and ideas between genres is apparent in 'The Loneliness of the Military Historian', which focuses on a female historian who justifies her fascination with war and who understands that others expect her to be a pacifist instead. She resembles Tony of *The Robber Bride*, who is also a military historian and who unsettles others, because they cannot reconcile who she is with what she does. The military historian of the poem does not judge her subjects, and the reader is therefore also reminded of *The Handmaid's Tale*, which concludes with the historian's plea to avoid passing moral judgement on totalitarian regimes.

In the 1990s, Atwood also published two compilations, *Selected Poems: 1965–1984* (1991) and *Eating Fire: Selected Poetry 1965–1995* (1998). She has only published one collection of poetry in the first decade of the twenty-first century, *The Door* (2007). This collection explores, amongst other things, the question of mortality, the art and craft of poetry, and includes poems that appear to be autobiographical. 'Butterfly' recounts the genesis of her father's interest in insects; 'My Mother Dwindles ...' appears to recount Atwood's own mother's slow decline. 'The Poet Has Come Back ...' suggests a return to poetry 'after decades of being virtuous instead'; the closing lines suggest 'the god of poets has two hands: / the dextrous, the sinister'. Atwood's critical writing *Negotiating with the Dead* and its meditations on writing are refigured here. 'Owl and Pussycat, Some Years Later' reflects on the hopes of youthful writers with plans to change the world, and the reality that art matters little in it after all, as well as a self-conscious realization that the 'worst is, now we're respectable. / We're in anthologies. We're taught in schools.' Atwood still has the power to surprise, however, with images that unsettle: 'In ten years, you'll be on a stamp, where anyone at all can lick you.' The sense of the body being licked cannot be divorced from the image itself being transferred onto a different metaphorical plane. Atwood's poets are ageing in 'The Poets Hang On' and 'Poetry Reading', and their art cannot hold back mortality or despair. These apparently personal poems are set against a larger political canvas; in 'War Photo', a beautiful woman is mourned even as she is aestheticized in death; in 'War Photo 2' the speaker recognizes that poetry cannot truly speak for those who are gone. This collection also contains Atwood's familiar return to the mythic; 'Another Visit to the Oracle', takes first a comic and then a serious tone, with the oracle tired of giving advice, which isn't heeded anyway. The oracle realizes that the seeker of knowledge who wants to know the future would rather have a happy story, but what she tells are 'dark stories / before and after they come true'. The collection ends with 'The Door', and the door of the title swings open and closed at intervals that surprise and startle the speaker. Within the gaps of these occurrences, life continues, children grow and move away, pets die, until the 'you' of the poem recognizes what to do: 'You confide yourself to the darkness. / You step in. / The door swings closed.' Atwood's use of 'confide' here, as in 'to entrust', offers a sense of desired closure, and there is something more than a little elegiac about this final image. The cover of the Virago edition shows a tinted photograph of (presumably) a young Atwood in front of a door – a door that is resolutely closed, offering both a sense of peeking in, and a sense that what is behind the door will stay firmly there. Atwood's sense of autobiographical disclosure is thus undermined and reinforced.

Chapter 4

Critical reception

As early as 1968, Atwood's poetry was catching the attention of literary critics such as W. H. New (who later became editor of *Canadian Literature*), though in an early survey of Canadian literature, she merited only a footnote. By the early 1970s, however, her poetry was featuring more prominently in reviews of Canadian literature, and, by the middle point of that decade, her novels had begun to receive sustained attention, too, and she was the subject of a special edition of *The Malahat Review*, a prominent Canadian literary journal.

From the first, critics have been interested in her depictions of female bodies and quests, power and gender politics, and her use of language. Carol P. Christ, for example, examined *Surfacing* as a spiritual quest only a few years after the novel was published. Atwood herself gave 'A Reply' to critics, including Christ, who were exploring *Surfacing* in an early volume of the feminist journal *Signs*, setting out her by now familiar views that literature is literature, not a treatise, and not a direct reflection of reality. However, her work has been consistently seen as referring to the world around her, whether that world is specifically associated with Canada, or whether it is more concerned with contemporary gender relations or with other political positions.

1970s and 1980s

What becomes obvious very quickly in reviewing the criticism on Atwood is the fact that the majority of Atwood scholars take a feminist approach, and this might be in part because she began writing at a time of raised feminist consciousness. The second-wave feminist movement offered a new critical paradigm, whereby women's concerns were seen as central, not peripheral, with consequences for women readers, women writers and the teachers of women's literature. Not only was male literature re-examined and its supposedly universal stance reconsidered, but earlier women's literature was reclaimed by feminists as of greater value than had previously been thought, and contemporary women writers were embraced for beginning to focus more explicitly on 'women's issues'. Atwood herself has often been cautious about being seen in these terms; nevertheless, her work has been frequently placed in the context of women's greater social and political power.

In 1971, Elaine Showalter argued that Atwood's work fitted into a feminist literary curriculum and might actually help to offer female students a new way of thinking about literature and themselves (such sentiments perhaps belatedly being reflected in Atwood's own short-story collection, *Moral Disorder*, where, in one story, the protagonist tries to understand her female teacher and herself through stories). In 1975, Annette Kolodny was using both *The Edible Woman* and *Surfacing* to explore the essence of feminist literary criticism. Donna Gerstenberger argued in 1976 that feminist writers were obliged to 'speak honestly about the lives of women and of men as women see them' and to 'make clear the inadequacy of past conceptions about reality, to alter what women (and men) have been taught to believe are the given facts of existence, to call out the conspiratorial lies' (Gerstenberger 144). Gerstenberger explores Atwood's use of language in *Surfacing*, focusing on the alienation of the narrator. Barbara Hill Rigney took another approach when she presented an implicitly comparative analysis of Atwood's work in *Madness and Sexual Politics in the Feminist Novel: Studies in Brontë, Woolf, Lessing and Atwood* (1978), which she followed with a single-author study on Atwood in 1987. In the former book, Rigney takes a feminist psychoanalytical approach, and considers Atwood a 'representative writer' (Rigney 3) – indicating the rise in Atwood's critical appeal at the end of the 1970s. Rigney focuses on *Surfacing* and on the narrator's 'alienated female consciousness' (Rigney 11). As is clear from this brief survey, Atwood's work was placed into a developing canon of contemporary women's literature and was viewed through the lens of the second-wave feminist movement throughout the 1970s.

The 1980s saw an explosion of Atwood criticism, with critical collections of essays and monographs appearing regularly, many of which explored Atwood's use of language or offered psychoanalytical approaches to her work. A number of the critics writing on Atwood in the 1980s went on to make their names as Atwoodian scholars, including Arnold E. Davidson, Sherrill Grace, Judith McCombs and Coral Ann Howells. Grace's *Violent Duality: A Study of Margaret Atwood* appeared in 1980. In it, Grace examines Atwood's use of symbols, archetypes and myths, focusing on the author's use of doubles and duplicity.

She argues that Atwood uses a style combining both realism and romance, and she reads Atwood partly through her own victim theory. Grace followed this book with a collection of essays in 1983, co-edited with Lorraine Weir; *Margaret Atwood: Language, Text and System* presents a structuralist and post-structuralist perspective on her work, exploring language patterns and disruptions. Arnold E. Davidson and Cathy N. Davidson edited *The Art of Margaret Atwood* (1981), a collection of essays that covers a wide range of approaches to Atwood's work and remains a key collection in relation to Atwood's early work. Unsurprisingly, these early edited collections are out of print but many can continue to be accessed through university libraries.

The 1980s also saw the formation of the Margaret Atwood Society, which began to publish a newsletter on Atwood in 1984. That same year, two monographs were published on Atwood that took her as their sole concern: Jerome H. Rosenberg's *Margaret Atwood* (in the Twayne series) and Frank Davey's *Margaret Atwood: A Feminist Poetics*. Rosenberg's text focuses primarily on her creative work, weaving in biographical details in places, mostly at the beginning and end of the book. Rosenberg offers close readings of her poetry in two chapters, and devotes one chapter to her fiction (*The Edible Woman* through to *Bodily Harm*) and one to her critical prose. The greater focus on her poetry reflects the fact that, for the first part of her career, Atwood was better known as a poet than as a novelist. In the final chapter, he explores Atwood's position in Canadian literature and delineates some of the critical controversies that surrounded her role as a public figure in Canada. The book is not markedly theorized but offers a solid grounding in close analysis of her early work.

Davey's book, like Rosenberg's, gives substantial space to Atwood's poetry and reads her first four novels as 'comedies'. By this he does not mean funny stories, but novels in which resolution is achieved. In other words, the novels start with 'social disruption', but end in a restored world (Davey 57). Davey argues, however, that Atwood's heroines must 'heal themselves', not society, and they are not always successful (Davey 57). He devotes a full chapter to *Life Before Man*, again more an indication of when the book was published than its enduring status in Atwood studies. He then presents what he calls an 'Atwood vocabulary', examining her use of technology, mirrors, the Gothic, mazes, refugees and totems, amongst other motifs. Several critics have followed Davey in focusing on these particular thematic concerns. Like Rosenberg, he also explores her short stories and her critical prose. His focus is on language, and although he subtitles his book 'a Feminist Poetics', he notes his own unease with Atwood's male–female dichotomies. This is as much a reflection of the time in which the text was written as it is a comment on Atwood's work.

Barbara Hill Rigney followed up her earlier work on Atwood with a slim monograph entitled, simply, *Margaret Atwood*, in 1987. This book marked a shift from considering Atwood primarily as a poet to considering the interrelationships between her poetry and her novels. For Rigney, Atwood is a writer who 'teaches mostly through negative examples' (Rigney 1). Her protagonists are not role models, but something more complex and human. Bearing in mind Atwood's own view on role models – 'I did not want to be a role model, I wanted to be a writer. One obviously would not have time for both' (*SW* 217) – this seems entirely appropriate. Rigney situates Atwood firmly as a feminist writer and as part of a female tradition. However, her reading of Atwood's apparent focus on 'sisterhood' (Rigney 10) is less clear now than perhaps it was in the 1980s, and more problematic than Rigney describes, particularly given the publication of *Cat's Eye* in 1988 which explicitly unpicks the idea of sisterhood or of female solidarity. Also in 1987, Beatrice Mendez-Egles published an edited collection entitled *Margaret Atwood: Reflection and Reality*. Essays within it explore rebellion, bodies and the image of the writer, amongst other topics.

Judith McCombs collected together a diverse range of articles on Atwood in 1988, entitling her collection *Critical Essays on Margaret Atwood*. She incorporated a number of reviews of Atwood's work from magazines and newspapers, offering critics the opportunity to explore and contrast the differing views of her oeuvre. Another major collection of essays appeared the same year. Edited by Kathryn Van Spanckeren and Jan Garden Castro, *Margaret Atwood: Vision and Forms* explicitly sets out to address a number of different concerns and critical positions on Atwood, including feminism, Atwood's use of the Gothic, her focus on ecology and politics. It is also the first major collection to include analysis of her visual artistic practices, an area that remains under-researched. Many of the contributors have gone on to produce further work on Atwood in the form of monographs and other critical collections. The collection includes fourteen essays, an interview with Atwood and a 'conversation' between Atwood and a group of students. Atwood also provides a short autobiographical foreword. The collection therefore presents a good example of Atwood criticism, in that it addresses the range of her work and also seeks to offer up Atwood's own voice against the voices of the critics.

1990s

In the 1990s, Atwood criticism expanded yet again, and the first major collection of interviews appeared, *Margaret Atwood: Conversations*, edited by Earl

Ingersoll; he later followed this up with an expanded version in 2006 entitled *Waltzing Again*, which is also the title of the interview he undertook with Atwood himself. Both are useful collections in that they present the opportunity to engage with Atwood's own views on her writing; they also reveal her caustic side at times, or perhaps impatience with the repetitive nature of the questions she is asked. In her interview with Ingersoll, Atwood claims: 'Let's not pretend however that an interview will necessarily result in any absolute and blinding revelations. Interviews too are an art form; that is to say, they indulge in the science of illusion' (234). If this caveat is kept in mind, one can explore the artistry of both the interviewer and the interviewee, and Atwood is a canny participant in these kinds of dialogue, withholding information as much as providing it.

The 1990s also saw the production of a comprehensive reference guide to Atwood's work, as well as two biographies of her. As noted in the introduction, neither of the biographies were authorized ones and in relation to both, Atwood appeared to express some hesitation, noting to the authors that since she was not 'dead yet', they were premature in their explorations. Nevertheless, both biographers set out to explore the image or life – perhaps both – of Canada's most famous author. *Margaret Atwood: A Biography*, by Nathalie Cooke, acts as a more traditional biography, whereas Rosemary Sullivan's *The Red Shoes: Margaret Atwood Starting Out*, is about Atwood's 'writing life', and is primarily focused on her early years as a writer, though it does, in its final chapter, move past this early focus.

Four monographs were published in 1993 alone that moved Atwood criticism forward substantially, because they offered detailed and individual attempts to explore specific aspects of Atwood's work. Eleonora Rao's *Strategies for Identity: The Fiction of Margaret Atwood* explores Atwood's work through the lens of postmodernism, generic disruptions and intertexuality. Rao argues that Atwood presents identity as process rather than product and in doing so, challenges notions of unity and subjectivity; in her view, Atwood uses duplicity as a strategic feminist play. Rao uses Lacanian psychoanalytic theory as well as the work of French feminists in relation to Atwood's work. Rao explores Atwood's work (mostly her novels) with different critical lenses, thus returning to texts in different contexts rather than presenting sustained analysis of individual texts in separate chapters.

Shannon Hengen's *Margaret Atwood's Power* also offers psychoanalytical readings of Atwood's work, focusing primarily on Atwood's exploration of power whilst also exploring narcissism and the recurrent imagery of mirrors. Indeed, her subtitle is *Mirrors, Reflections and Images in Select Fiction and Poetry*. Hengen concentrates on Atwood's fiction with only brief forays into her poetry. She suggests that Atwood's readership is primarily an educated one, but that, within this group, there are still inequalities of power – which Atwood's work taps into and reveals. Specially, Hengen argues that power can be determined by how individuals (or countries) are defined: 'Canada, for example, is a country often defined as that-which-is-North-American-but-not-American, and female is that-which-is-human-but-not-male; the difference between the terms is power' (Hengen 12). Hengen also argues that Atwood writes 'at the thematic juncture of socialism and feminism' (Hengen 15) and that she recognizes the need for her female characters to be aware of themselves as part of a wider cultural history in order to gain full access to power. Of course, what becomes very interesting in relation to Atwood is that her manipulations of power become more overt in her later work – work that was published subsequent to Hengen's own publication. The careful reader will nonetheless be able to explore the power of Zenia in *The Robber Bride*, or Grace in *Alias Grace*, in relation to Hengen's work.

There are some similar concerns in J. Brooks Bouson's *Brutal Choreographies: Oppositional Strategies and Narrative Design in the Novels of Margaret Atwood*. Bouson focuses on Atwood's use of femininity as a construct. Like Hengen, Bouson explores Atwood's work through psychoanalytic theory as well as feminism, though she focuses only on Atwood's first seven novels (*The Edible Woman* through to *Cat's Eye*). In seeking out connections between the novels, Bouson argues that Atwood's exploration of power resides not just in male–female relationships, but also female–female power struggles (including the mother–daughter struggle). Bouson reads Atwood as a subversive author who unpicks the fantasy of romantic love and who engages with a range of feminist stances in her novels, from proto-feminism in the earliest novel to cultural feminism, postfeminism and feminist backlash.

Sharon Rose Wilson's monograph on Atwood, *Margaret Atwood's Fairy-Tale Sexual Politics*, is also the first to explore her artistic practices in any depth. It builds on her earlier essay in Van Spanckeren and Castro's edited collection which also linked Atwood's pictorial art with her literary artistry. Wilson explores Atwood's use of the fairy tale motif against a range of other sources; her work is supported by sustained archival research at the Thomas Fisher Rare Book Library at the University of Toronto, which holds Atwood's papers. It is a measure of Atwood's popularity with critics that she attracts this kind of specific focus at the same time that more wide-ranging studies are being published.

Colin Nicholson's edited collection *Margaret Atwood: Writing and Subjectivity* followed in 1994. Nicholson drew his contributors from across North America and Europe. He frames his introduction and his own essay around postcolonialism, whereas the other essays explore a number of (related) issues, including gender, fictive autobiographical gestures, history and narrative. The collection includes three essays focusing on Atwood's poetry, six essays covering specific novels and three on Atwood's short stories as well as an essay that ranges across several novels. Lorraine York's edited collection, *Various Atwoods*, is explicit in its focus on Atwood's later works, including her short stories; again York is able to gather together a range of eminent Atwood scholars to produce this collection of twelve essays. An exploration of the filmed version of *The Handmaid's Tale* is also included, as well as, for the first time, an essay on *The Robber Bride*.

Sonia Mycak's *In Search of the Split Subject: Psychoanalysis, Phenomenology, and the Novels of Margaret Atwood* was published in 1996 and, as the title suggests, takes a psychoanalytical approach to her work. It presents close readings of six novels (*The Edible Woman* through to *The Robber Bride*) and explores the importance of the divided self in Atwood's novels. It comes as something of a surprise that Atwood's most heavily critiqued novels, *Surfacing* and *The Handmaid's Tale*, are not given sustained treatment, but Mycak includes an appendix which tries to address the omission. She argues that the two excluded novels are fundamentally different from the rest of Atwood's oeuvre and therefore cannot be placed within the same critical framework. She also suggests that because *The Handmaid's Tale* is best read as a feminist or dystopian text, it cannot be explored fully within her own framework. Similarly, she argues that *Surfacing* is best read as a quest narrative, and again therefore dismisses it from further consideration. Mycak includes a glossary of terms, including Castration Complex, Desire, Drive, Ego, Imaginary, Mirror Stage, Oedipal Complex, Real, Symbolic, Symptom and Unconscious in order to guide the reader through her critical apparatus.

In 1996, Coral Ann Howells published her single-author survey of Atwood's work, entitled, simply, *Margaret Atwood*. She later updated this in 2005 with a second edition, to take into account new work by the author. Howells' focus is on Atwood's use of language and methods of storytelling, her cognizance of power and her texts' open-endedness. In this second edition Howells argues that Atwood's novels 'are characterised by their refusals to invoke any final authority as their open endings resist conclusiveness, offering instead hesitation, absence or silence while hovering on the verge of new possibilities' (Howells 2005, 10). Jerome Rosenberg's book in the Twayne series was updated in 1999 by Karen Stein, with the new book title *Margaret Atwood Revisited*. It is testament to the continued interest in Atwood's writing – as well as her productivity – that publishers seek second editions to critical texts that are no longer in print. Moreover, there are a number of books that relate to the teaching of Atwood's work. The edited collection *Approaches to Teaching Atwood's The Handmaid's Tale and Other Works* (ed. Wilson, Friedman and Hengen), published by the Modern Language Association in 1996, is perhaps the strongest of this field, presenting, as it does, not only background information, but a section on approaches and pedagogy. Whilst focusing on *The Handmaid's Tale*, the book also ranges much further, including criticism on Atwood's poetry, some short stories and a variety of other novels.

Atwood criticism in the twenty-first century

Atwood's work continues to receive substantial attention in the twenty-first century, including in texts that explore her work in relation to other women writers, other Canadian writers or other postmodern writers (and of course these designations overlap, as in Howells' *Contemporary Canadian Women's Fiction: Refiguring Identities*, published in 2003); as well as other thematic and critical foci, such as postcolonialism (in, for example, Jacqueline Bardolph's edited collection *Telling Stories: Postcolonial Short Fiction in English*) or dystopian fiction. Her work has been explored in relation to escape in feminist fiction (particularly *Surfacing*, *Lady Oracle* and *The Handmaid's Tale* in Macpherson's *Women's Movement*, 2000) and law and literature (*Alias Grace* in Macpherson's *Courting Failure*, 2007); and her attention to older women (*The Blind Assassin*, *The Robber Bride* in Phyllis Sternberg Perrakis' edited collection *Adventures of the Spirit*, 2007), to name but a few of the books that explore her work in relation to other women writers.

At the same time, critics continue to publish books that take her as their sole focus. Fiona Tolan's monograph *Margaret Atwood: Feminism and Fiction* includes an examination of Atwood's novels up to and including *Oryx and Crake* and, as the title suggests, explores Atwood's work in relation to its various feminist impulses. Ellen McWilliams' *Margaret Atwood and the Female Bildungsroman* reads Atwood's work (including unpublished materials) through the lens of the Bildungsroman, or the narrative of a young person and his or her education and development.

In addition to single-authored texts, there is a plethora of edited collections that have been published in the twenty-first century. Reingard M. Nischik edited a wide-ranging book, *Margaret Atwood: Works and Impact*, which was published in 2000; the book was conceived as a response to Atwood's 60th birthday, which had taken place in November 1999. In it, Nischik includes standard scholarly articles as well as personal testimonies, photographs of Atwood and, at the end, a series of cartoons by or about her. The book is divided into sections on her life and status (with essays on biography, celebrity and canonization); her work (with separate review essays on her novels, short fiction, poetry and criticism); and approaches to her work (with essays on Atwood's genres, her use of narrative, and her exploration of, amongst other things, gender, nationalism and mythology). The final section, entitled 'Creativity – Transmission – Reception' is the least scholarly in that it offers space to individuals to respond to Atwood as a writer, or as a woman or as someone with whom to work. It even includes a section entitled 'Margaret Atwood in Statements by Fellow Writers', some of which were commissioned especially for the volume. Part scholarly, part homage, the book itself includes some useful interventions in Atwood studies (not least because it collects together a number of eminent Atwood scholars) whilst also directing some of its energies to a non-academic audience.

A more consistently scholarly edition, *The Cambridge Companion to Margaret Atwood*, edited by Coral Ann Howells, was published in 2006. This collection of twelve essays, introduced and edited by Coral Ann Howells, is a welcome addition to the scholarship on Margaret Atwood, and most of the essays attain a very high standard. This is not surprising, given that Howells has brought together a range of well-known Atwoodian critics, including Lorraine York, Shannon Hengen, Sharon R. Wilson, Marta Dvorak, Reingard M. Nischik and Eleonora Rao, to explore Atwood's work. Aimed at an undergraduate market, the essays are relatively jargon-free and concise, whilst ranging over the whole of Atwood's oeuvre up to and including *Oryx and Crake*. Some of the essays form interesting links; in one example, an essay on power and politics by Pilar Somacarrera is followed immediately by an essay by Madeleine Davies on female bodies that reinterprets Atwood's use of power through the visual display and surveillance of women. These connections offer alternative but connected ways of viewing Atwood's work. The inevitable overlap in chapters that explore the same texts becomes a benefit of the collection; the committed student has an opportunity to read Atwood's work whilst engaging with a variety of perspectives on the same texts. The collection begins with an Atwood chronology and a helpful introductory essay, followed by David Staines' essay on Atwood and her Canadian context. York's essay on biography/autobiography focuses on Atwood as a text herself, in her role as a Canadian celebrity. In her essay on politics and power, Somacarrera reads across genres, identifying companion pieces, such as 'Notes towards a Poem that Can never be Written' and *Bodily Harm*, a practice that might encourage students to find other resonances. Davies' essay on the body focuses on *Lady Oracle*, *Cat's Eye* and *The Blind Assassin*, whereas Hengen's essay on environmentalism ranges across non-fiction, fiction and poetry. This is followed by

Coomi Vevaini's essay on Atwood and history that links her work to Salman Rushdie. Rao's essay takes three novels from three decades in order to explore home and nation, and Dvorak's essay on humour closely reads a range of texts, including the short story 'Significant Moments in the Life of My Mother'. Each essay in the collection is relatively short. This tight structure works best when authors take a more limited approach in selecting texts for closer reading, as Nischik does in relation to the short story. By far the best essay is Howells' own, on dystopia, which presents clear and informed readings of *The Handmaid's Tale* and *Oryx and Crake*. The collection concludes with an exploration of blindness and survival by Wilson. This collection of essays offers a number of readings of Atwood's most important works, as well as an exploration of her recurrent fictional and poetic preoccupations.

Sharon Rose Wilson's edited collection *Margaret Atwood's Textual Assassinations* focuses on Atwood's work of the 1980s and 1990s. In her introduction, Wilson argues that '[i]t is no accident that the words *strange* and *stranger*, along with *alien* and *alienation*, *murder* or *assassination*, *survival*, and *trickster* recur in the article titles or the essays themselves' (Wilson xii) and this list gives a clear indication of the kinds of analysis that follow. The essays take postcolonial and postmodern stances towards Atwood's work, and they analyse not only her novels, but also her shorter fictions, poetry and short-short stories, often exploring her work in a metafictional context. Wilson contributes two essays out of the ten that make up the collection, as well as the introduction.

Finally, no survey of the critical literature on Atwood would be complete without referencing the Margaret Atwood Society. In 2007, a new journal was established, *Margaret Atwood Studies*, coming out of the society's Newsletter, which had been published since 1984. As noted in the introduction, over 100 pieces of scholarly work are regularly produced in a single year on Atwood, and collected annually in the publication under the title 'Current Atwood Checklist'. In addition to the scholarly works that are listed, the checklist offers information on Atwood's publications, interviews, adaptations, quotations, news stories and reviews; in 2007, the separately published *Margaret Atwood Reference Guide* was updated to include the years 1988–2006.

Thus, it appears that critical interest in Atwood continues to grow and expand, and the likelihood is that as Atwood herself adds to her oeuvre, with new novels and collections of poetry, short stories (including short-short stories) and essays, as well as miscellaneous writing, Atwood studies will continue to thrive. She is amongst the most important contemporary women writers, and critics are still discovering new ways to address and respond to her work.

Notes

1 Life

1 The interview with Atwood was conducted on 8 August 2007, at L'Espresso Bar Mercurio, Toronto. Any unattributed quotations derive from the interview I undertook with her. Thanks are extended to Rachael Walters for her excellent transcription of the interview.

2 See *Margaret Atwood Studies* 1.2 (December 2007); the Margaret Atwood Society annually collects information on Atwood's publications and publications on Atwood.

3 See www.owtoad.com, last accessed 20 February 2008.

4 Indeed, such is the critical swing away from autobiography, that perusal of the Atwood archives in the summer of 2007 led to my own critical unease. Occasionally I would uncover childhood correspondence, touchingly preserved, and it was in those moments that as a literary scholar I felt some disquiet, examining home-made 'books' and letters to and from grandparents. If everything is material to writers, is it appropriate that everything is material to scholars, too? Yet Atwood placed these items in the archive, and therefore must be assumed to be happy that they are there. Of these personal effects there are actually only a few, and the correspondence that is in the archives is primarily related to specific working projects. Ironically, this also became a disappointment, even though the notes on the archive quite specifically state in the opening description of the materials that this will be the case: 'Most of the correspondence in the collection relates to the editing and publication of literary works. Some personal letters are included in the earlier correspondence. Personal correspondence after 1967 is restricted. There is very little memorabilia or printed material documenting Atwood's career. The focus of the collection is almost completely on Atwood's literary work. Biographical material exists only for the pre 1967 years.'

5 See http://archives.cbc.ca/IDC-1-68-1494-10058/arts_Entertainment/margaret_atwood/clip5, last accessed 24 February 2008.

2 Contexts

1 See *CanText: The Newsletter of the BACS Literature Group* 2.2 (March 2000): 1–3 for the results of both surveys.

2 I first came across this assertion at the British Association for Canadian Studies conference in 1998, and two Swedish colleagues, Ingela Aberg and Jonas Stier, later confirmed it. A module on Atwood that I previously taught at the University of Central Lancashire could be considered as part of either the English Literature programme or the American Studies programme, depending on a Combined Honours student's needs. Even in the USA, Atwood's nationality is rarely marked by teachers or lecturers, and indeed her most frequently taught text is set in Gilead, the former USA, which may account, somewhat, for this failure to acknowledge nationality.

3 See www.whatisstephenharperreading.ca/the_story_behind_this_website.html, accessed 11 February 2008.

4 In the USA and Canada, her collection *Moving Targets: Writing with Intent* covers a shorter range but includes much of the same material; thirty-five of the essays in *Moving Targets* are also published in *Curious Pursuits* (though occasionally with different titles). Although there are some differences between the collections, there is too much overlap to consider both of them in detail, and *Curious Pursuits* is the most readily accessible in the UK.

3 Works

1 Taken from a transcript of a talk given by Atwood in May 1995 at a gathering of the Toronto Council of Teachers of English, www.owtoad.com/q_and_a.pdf, accessed 22 November 2008.

2 Many critics, including Jerome Rosenberg, confuse Joan's fake death with fake suicide. In fact, the thought of suicide appals Joan, who was hoping to have her death characterized as one of misadventure.

3 See, for example, David Ketterer (dystopia), Janet L. Larson (prophecy), Stephanie Barbé Hammer (satire), Heidi Macpherson (slave narrative), Maria Lauret (also slave narrative), and Madonne Miner (romance), amongst others.

4 In her exploration of Atwood's shorter fiction, Nischik touches on *Bottle* (2004), a limited-edition book which was produced for the Hay-on-Wye Festival; the stories collected there were eventually published in *The Tent* and are thus not separately considered here.

5 The UK version of the book, published by Vintage, omits 'The War in the Bathroom' and 'Rape Fantasies' and includes two stories not in the original Canadian version, 'The Sin Eater' and 'Betty'. The latter two stories were published in some versions of *Bluebeard's Egg*. See, for example, Davey's explication of the stories. I will be using the British version here.

Further reading

Margaret Atwood's works

Novels

The Edible Woman. 1969. London: Virago, 1992.
Surfacing. 1972. London: Virago, 1991.
Lady Oracle. 1976. London: Virago, 1992.
Life Before Man. 1979. London: Vintage, 1996.
Bodily Harm. 1981. London: Virago, 1991.
The Handmaid's Tale. 1985. London: Virago, 1992.
Cat's Eye. 1988. London: Virago, 1990.
The Robber Bride. London: Bloomsbury, 1993.
Alias Grace. London: Bloomsbury, 1996.
The Blind Assassin. London: Bloomsbury, 2000.
Oryx and Crake. London: Bloomsbury, 2003.
The Year of the Flood. London: Bloomsbury, 2009.

Short stories and shorter works

Dancing Girls and Other Stories. 1977. London: Vintage, 1996.
Bluebeard's Egg and Other Stories. 1983. London: Vintage, 1996.
Murder in the Dark. 1983. London: Virago, 1994.
Good Bones. London: Virago, 1992.
Wilderness Tips. 1991. London: Bloomsbury, 1995.
The Penelopiad. Edinburgh: Canongate, 2005.
Moral Disorder. London: Bloomsbury, 2006.
The Tent. London: Bloomsbury, 2006.

Poetry

Double Persephone. Toronto: Hawkshead Press, 1961.
The Circle Game. Toronto: House of Anansi, 1966.
The Animals in That Country. Oxford: Oxford University Press, 1968.
The Journals of Susanna Moodie. Oxford: Oxford University Press, 1970.

Procedures for Underground. Oxford: Oxford University Press, 1970.
Power Politics. Toronto: House of Anansi, 1971.
You Are Happy. Oxford: Oxford University Press, 1974.
Two-Headed Poems. Oxford: Oxford University Press, 1978.
True Stories. Oxford: Oxford University Press, 1981.
Interlunar. Oxford: Oxford University Press, 1984.
Morning in the Burned House. Toronto: McClelland & Stewart, 1995.
Eating Fire: Selected Poetry 1965–1995. London: Virago, 1998.
The Door. London: Virago, 2007.

Non-fiction

Survival: A Thematic Guide to Canadian Literature. Toronto: McClelland &
        Stewart, 1972.
Days of the Rebels 1815–1840. Toronto: Natural Science of Canada, 1977.
Second Words: Selected Critical Prose. Toronto: Anansi, 1982.
Strange Things: The Malevolent North in Canadian Literature. Oxford: Clarendon
        Press, 1995.
Two Solicitudes: Conversations, with Victor-Lévy Beaulieu. Toronto: McClelland
        & Stewart, 1998.
Negotiating with the Dead: A Writer on Writing. Cambridge: Cambridge
        University Press, 2002.
Moving Targets: Writing with Intent. Toronto: Anansi, 2004.
Curious Pursuits: Occasional Writing 1970–2005. London: Virago, 2005.
Payback: Debt as Metaphor and the Shadow Side of Wealth. London: Bloomsbury,
        2008.

Children's books

Up in the Tree. Toronto: McClelland & Stewart, 1978.
Anna's Pet, with Joyce Barkhouse. Halifax, NS: Lorimer, 1980.
For the Birds, with Shelly Tanaka. Toronto: Douglas & McIntyre, 1990.
Princess Prunella and the Purple Peanut. New York: Workman Publishing, 1995.
Rude Ramsay and the Roaring Radishes. Toronto: Key Porter Books, 2003.
Bashful Bob and Doleful Dorinda. Toronto: Key Porter Books, 2004.

Further reading sections

The Edible Woman

Bouson, J. Brooks. *Brutal Choreographies: Oppositional Strategies and Narrative
        Design in the Novels of Margaret Atwood*. Amherst: University of
        Massachusetts Press, 1993.

Friedan, Betty. *The Feminine Mystique*. 1963. London: Penguin Books, 1992.
Griffith, Margaret. 'Verbal Terrain in the Novels of Margaret Atwood', *Critique* 21.3 (1980): 85–93.
MacLulich, T. D. 'Atwood's Adult Fairy Tale: Levi-Strauss, Bettelheim, and *The Edible Woman*', in McCombs (ed.), *Critical Essays*, 179–97.
Palumbo, Alice M. 'On the Border: Margaret Atwood's Novels', in Nischik (ed.), *Margaret Atwood*, 73–86.
White, Roberta. 'Margaret Atwood: Reflections in a Convex Mirror', in Mickey Pearlman (ed.), *Canadian Women Writing Fiction*. Jackson: University Press of Mississippi, 1993, 53–59.
Woodcock, George. 'Margaret Atwood: Poet as Novelist', in McCombs (ed.), *Critical Essays*, 90–104.

Surfacing

Bjerring, Nancy E. 'The Problem of Language in Margaret Atwood's *Surfacing*', *Queen's Quarterly* 83 (1976): 597–612.
Bouson, J. Brooks. *Brutal Choreographies: Oppositional Strategies and Narrative Design in the Novels of Margaret Atwood*. Amherst: University of Massachusetts Press, 1993.
Frye, Northrop. *The Bush Garden: Essays on the Canadian Imagination*. Toronto: Anansi, 1971.
Larkin, Joan. 'Soul Survivor', in McCombs (ed.), *Critical Essays*, 48–52.
Schaub, Danielle. ' "I am a Place": Internalised Landscape and Female Subjectivity in Margaret Atwood's *Surfacing*', in Danielle Schaub (ed.), *Mapping Canadian Cultural Space: Essays on Canadian Literature*. Jerusalem: The Hebrew University Magnes Press, 2000.

Lady Oracle

Cawelti, John G. *Adventure, Mystery, and Romance*. Chicago: University of Chicago Press, 1976.
Howells, Coral Ann. *Margaret Atwood*. 2nd edn. Houndmills: Palgrave, 2005.
Russ, Joanna. 'Somebody's Trying to Kill Me and I Think It's My Husband: The Modern Gothic', *Journal of Popular Culture* 4 (1973): 666–91.
Sedgwick, Eve Kosofsky. *The Coherence of Gothic Conventions*, 1980. New York: Methuen, 1986.
Vincent, Sybill Korff. 'The Mirror and the Cameo: Margaret Atwood's Comic/ Gothic Novel, *Lady Oracle*', in Fleenor (ed.), *The Female Gothic*. Montreal: Eden Press, 1983, 153–63.

Life Before Man

Davey, Frank. *Margaret Atwood: A Feminist Poetics*. Vancouver: Talonbooks, 1984.

Howells, Coral Ann. *Margaret Atwood*. 2nd edn. Houndmills: Palgrave, 2005.
Irvine, Lorna. 'Murder and Mayhem: Margaret Atwood Deconstructs',
    Contemporary Literature 29.2 (1988): 265–76.

Bodily Harm

Hansen, Elaine Tuttle. 'Fiction and (Post) Feminism in Atwood's *Bodily Harm*',
    Novel 19.1 (1985): 5–21.
Howells, Coral Ann. 'Worlds Alongside: Contradictory Discourses in the
    Fiction of Alice Munro and Margaret Atwood', in Robert Kroetsch
    and Reingard M. Nischik (eds.), *Gaining Ground: European Critics on
    Canadian Literature*. Edmonton: NeWest Press, 1985, 121–36.
    Margaret Atwood. 2nd edn. Houndmills: Palgrave, 2005.
Irvine, Lorna. 'The Here and Now of *Bodily Harm*', in Van Spanckeren and Castro
    (eds.), *Margaret Atwood*, 85–100.
Rubenstein, Roberta. 'Pandora's Box and Female Survival: Margaret Atwood's
    Bodily Harm', in McCombs (ed.), *Critical Essays*, 259–275.

The Handmaid's Tale

Hammer, Stephanie Barbé. 'The World as it will be? Satire and Technology
    of Power in *The Handmaid's Tale*', *Modern Language Studies* 20.2
    (1990): 39–49.
Kaler, Anne K. ' "A Sister Dipped in Blood": Satiric Inversion of the Formation
    Techniques of Women Religious in Margaret Atwood's Novel *The
    Handmaid's Tale*', *Christianity and Literature* 38.2 (1989): 43–63.
Ketterer, David. 'Margaret Atwood's *The Handmaid's Tale*: A Contextual
    Dystopia', *Science Fiction Studies* 16.2 (48) (1989): 209–17.
Larson, Janet L. 'Margaret Atwood and the Future of Prophecy', *Religion and
    Literature* 21.1 (1989): 27–61.
Lauret, Maria. *Liberating Literature: Feminist Fiction in America*.
    London: Routledge, 1994.
LeBihan, Jill. '*The Handmaid's Tale*, *Cat's Eye*, and *Interlunar*: Margaret Atwood's
    Feminist (?) Futures (?)', in Coral Ann Howells and Lynette Hunter
    (eds.), *Narrative Strategies in Canadian Literature: Feminism and Post-
    Colonialism*. New York: Taylor & Francis, 1991, 93–107.
Macpherson, Heidi Slettedahl. *Women's Movement: Escape as Transgression in
    North American Feminist Fiction*. Amsterdam: Rodopi, 2000.
Miner, Madonne. ' "Trust Me": Reading the Romance Plot in Margaret Atwood's
    The Handmaid's Tale', *Twentieth-Century Literature: A Scholarly and
    Critical Journal* 37.2 (1991): 148–68.
Rubenstein, Roberta. 'Nature and Nurture in Dystopia: *The Handmaid's Tale*', in
    Van Spanckeren and Castro (eds.), *Margaret Atwood*, 101–12.

Cat's Eye

Foucault, Michel. 'Panopticism', in Alan Sheridan (trans.), *Discipline and Punish: The Birth of the Prison*, 1975. London: Penguin, 1991, 195–228.
Hite, Molly. 'Optics and Autobiography in Margaret Atwood's *Cat's Eye*', *Twentieth Century Literature* 41.2 (1995): 135–59.
Howells, Coral Ann. *Margaret Atwood*. 2nd edn. Houndmills: Palgrave, 2005.
Ingersoll, Earl G. *Waltzing Again: New and Selected Conversations with Margaret Atwood*. Princeton, NJ: Ontario Review Press, 2006.

The Robber Bride

Bouson, J. Brooks. 'Slipping Sideways into the Dreams of Women: The Female Dream Work of Power Feminism in Margaret Atwood's *The Robber Bride*', *LIT: Literature Interpretation Theory* 6.3–4 (1995): 149–66.
Chernin, Kim. *Womansize: The Tyranny of Slenderness*, 1981. London: The Women's Press, 1989.
Perrakis, Phyllis Sternberg. 'Atwood's *The Robber Bride*: The Vampire as Intersubjective Catalyst', *Mosaic* 30.3 (1997): 151–68.
Potts, Donna L. ' "The Old Maps are Dissolving": Intertextuality and Identity in Atwood's *The Robber Bride*', *Tulsa Studies in Women's Literature* 18.2 (1999): 281–98.

Alias Grace

Atwood, Margaret. 'In Search of *Alias Grace*: On Writing Canadian Historical Fiction', *Curious Pursuits*. London: Virago, 2005, 209–29.
Howells, Coral Ann. *Contemporary Canadian Women's Fiction: Refiguring Identities*. Houndmills: Palgrave Macmillan, 2003.
  Margaret Atwood. 2nd edn. Houndmills: Palgrave, 2005.
Hutchison, Lorna. 'The Book Reads Well: Atwood's *Alias Grace* and the Middle Voice', *Pacific Coast Philology* 38 (2003): 40–59.
Knelman, Judith. 'Can We Believe what theNewspapers tell us? Missing Links in *Alias Grace*', *University of Toronto Quarterly: A Canadian Journal of the Humanities* 68.2 (1999): 677–86.
Macpherson, Heidi Slettedahl. *Courting Failure: Women and the Law in Twentieth-Century Literature*. Akron: University of Akron Press, 2007.
  Women's Movement: Escape as Transgression in North American Feminist Fiction. Amsterdam: Rodopi, 2000.
March, Cristie. 'Crimson Silks and New Potatoes: The Heteroglossic Power of the Object in Atwood's *Alias Grace*', *Studies in Canadian Literature* 22.2 (1997): 66–82.

Murray, Jennifer. 'Historical Figures and Paradoxical Patterns: The Quilting Motif in Margaret Atwood's *Alias Grace*', *Studies in Canadian Literature* 26.1 (2001): 65–83.

Stanley, Sandra Kumamoto. 'The Eroticism of Class and the Enigma of Margaret Atwood's *Alias Grace*', *Tulsa Studies in Women's Literature* 22.2 (2003): 371–86.

Wilson, Sharon Rose. *Margaret Atwood's Textual Assassinations: Recent Poetry and Fiction*. Columbus: Ohio State University Press, 2003.

The Blind Assassin

Bouson, J. Brooks. ' "A Commemoration of Wounds Endured and Resented": Margaret Atwood's *The Blind Assassin* as Feminist Memoir', *Critique* 44.3 (2003): 251–69.

Dancygier, Barbara. 'Narrative Anchors and the Processes of Story Construction: The Case of Margaret Atwood's *The Blind Assassin*', *Style* 41.2 (2007): 133–52.

Howells, Coral Ann. *Margaret Atwood*. 2nd edn. Houndmills: Palgrave, 2005.

Ingersoll, Earl. 'Waiting for the End: Closure in Margaret Atwood's *The Blind Assassin*', *Studies in the Novel* 35.4 (2003): 543–58.

Staels, Hilde. 'Atwood's Specular Narrative: *The Blind Assassin*', *English Studies* 2 (2004): 147–60.

Oryx and Crake and The Year of the Flood

Atwood, Margaret. 'Writing Oryx and Crake', *Curious Pursuits*, 321–3.

Barzilai, Shuli. "Tell My Story": Remembrance and Revenge in Atwood's *Oryx and Crake* and Shakespeare's *Hamlet*', *Critique* 50.1 (2008): 87–110.

Bouson, J. Brooks. ' "It's Game Over Forever": Atwood's Satiric Vision of a Bioengineered Posthuman Future in *Oryx and Crake*', *The Journal of Commonwealth Literature* 39 (2004): 139–56.

Cole, Amanda. 'In Retrospect: Writing and Reading *Oryx and Crake*', *Philament: An Online Journal of the Arts and Culture* 6 (July 2005): www.arts.usyd.edu.au/publications/philament/issue6_contents.htm, accessed 15 August 2009.

DiMarco, Danette. 'Paradice Lost, Paradise Regained: *homo faber* and the Makings of a New Beginning in *Oryx and Crake*', *Papers on Language and Literature* 41 (2005): 170–95.

Halliwell, Martin. 'Awaiting the Perfect Storm', in Ingersoll (ed.), *Waltzing Again*, 251–64.

Howells, Coral Ann. *Margaret Atwood*. 2nd edn. Houndmills: Palgrave, 2005.

Wagner, Erica. 'The Conversation: Margaret Atwood', *The Times* [London], Review Section, 3, 15 August 2009.

Short stories

Davey, Frank. 'Alternate Stories: The Short Fiction of Audrey Thomas and
  Margaret Atwood', *Canadian Literature* 109 (1986): 5–14.
  Margaret Atwood: A Feminist Poetics. Vancouver: Talonbooks, 1984.
Godard, Barbara. 'Tales within Tales: Margaret Atwood's Folk Narratives',
  Canadian Literature 109 (1986): 57–84.
Nischik, Reingard M. 'Margaret Atwood's Short Stories and Shorter Fictions', in
  Howells (ed.), *The Cambridge Companion*,145–60.
Sturgess, Charlotte. 'Margaret Atwood's Short Fiction', in Nischik (ed.), *Margaret
  Atwood*, 87–96.

Poetry

Beyer, Charlotte. 'Feminist Revisionist Mythology and Female Identity in
  Margaret Atwood's Recent Poetry', *Literature and Theology* 14.3
  (2000): 276–98.
Hönnighausen, Lothar. 'Margaret Atwood's Poetry 1966–95', in Nischik (ed.),
  Margaret Atwood, 97–119.
Johnston, Gordon. ' "The Ruthless Story and the Future Tense" in Margaret
  Atwood's Circe/Mud Poems', *Studies in Canadian Literature* 5
  (1980): 167–76.
Klappert, Peter. 'I Want, I Don't Want: The Poetry of Margaret Atwood',
  Gettysburg Review 3.1 (1990): 217–30.
Ladousse, Gillian Porter. 'Gender and Language in Margaret Atwood's Poetry',
  Commonwealth Essays and Studies 20.1 (1997): 10–16.
Oates, Joyce Carol. 'My Mother Would Rather Skate Than Scrub Floors', Ingersoll
  (ed.), *Waltzing Again*, 37–42.
Woolf, Virginia. *A Room of One's Own*, 1929. London: Penguin, 2002.

Contexts section

Billingham, Susan, and Danielle Fuller. 'Can Lit(e): Fit for Export?', *Essays on
  Canadian Writing* 71 (2000): 76–112.
Castro, Jan Garden. 'An Interview with Margaret Atwood', in Van Spanckeren and
  Castro (eds.), *Margaret Atwood*, 215–32.
Corse, Sarah M. *Nationalism and Literature: The Politics of Culture in Canada and
  the United States*. Cambridge: Cambridge University Press, 1997.
Frye, Northrop. *The Bush Garden: Essays on the Canadian Imagination*.
  Toronto: Anansi, 1971.
  'Conclusion', in Karl F. Klinck. (ed.), *Literary History of Canada: Canadian
  Literature in English*. Totonto: University of Toronto Press, 1965,
  821–49.

Grace, Sherrill. *Violent Duality: A Study of Margaret Atwood*. Montreal: Vehicule Press, 1980.

Graves, Robert. *The White Goddess: A Historical Grammar of Poetic Myth*. London: Faber & Faber, 1948.

Hancock, Geoff. 'Tightrope-Walking over Niagara Falls', in Ingersoll (ed.), *Waltzing Again*, 90–118.

Irvine, Lorna. 'A Psychological Journey: Mothers and Daughters in English Canadian Fiction', in Cathy N. Davidson and E. M. Broner (eds.), *The Lost Tradition: Mothers and Daughters in Literature*. New York: Frederick Ungar, 1980.

Kertzer, Jonathan. *Worrying the Nation: Imagining a National Literature in English-Canada*. Toronto: University of Toronto Press, 1998.

Kroetsch, Robert. *The Lovely Treachery of Words: Essays Selected and New*. Toronto: Oxford University Press, 1989.

Loriggio, Francesco. 'The Question of the Corpus: Ethnicity and Canadian Literature', in John Moss (ed.), *Future Indicative. Literary Theory and Canadian Literature*. Ottawa: University of Ottawa Press, 1987, 53–68.

Pache, Walter. ' "A Certain Frivolity": Margaret Atwood's Literary Criticism', in Nischik (ed.), *Margaret Atwood*, 120–35.

Rosenthal, Caroline. 'Canonizing Atwood: Her Impact on Teaching in the US, Canada, and Europe', in Nischik (ed.), *Margaret Atwood*, 41–56.

Sandler, Linda. 'A Question of Metamorphosis', in Ingersoll (ed.), *Waltzing Again*, 18–36.

Staines, David. 'Margaret Atwood in her Canadian Context', in Howells (ed.), *The Cambridge Companion*, 12–27.

Templin, Charlotte. 'Tyler's Literary Reputation', in Dale Salwak (ed.), *Anne Tyler as Novelist*. Iowa City: University of Iowa Press, 1994, 175–96.

Van Spanckeren, Kathryn, and Jan Garden Castro (eds.). *Margaret Atwood: Vision and Forms*. Carbondale: Southern Illinois University Press, 1988.

Wilson, Sharon Rose. *Margaret Atwood's Fairy-Tale Sexual Politics*. Jackson: University of Mississippi Press, 1993.

York, Lorraine. *Literary Celebrity in Canada*. Toronto: University of Toronto Press, 2007.

Criticism section

Atwood, Margaret. 'A Reply', *Signs* 2.2 (1976): 340–1.

Bardolph, Jacqueline. *Telling Stories: Postcolonial Short Fiction in English*. Amsterdam: Rodopi, 2001.

Christ, Carol P. 'Margaret Atwood: The Surfacing of Women's Spiritual Quest and Vision', *Signs* 2.2 (1976): 316–30.

Gerstenberger, Donna. 'Conceptions Literary and Otherwise: Women Writers and the Modern Imagination', *Novel: A Forum on Fiction* 9.2 (1976): 141–50.

Kolodny, Annette. 'Some Notes on Defining a "Feminist Literary Criticism"', *Critical Inquiry* 2.1 (1975): 75–92.

New, William H. 'A Well Spring of Magna: Modern Canadian Writing', *Twentieth Century Literature* 14.3 (1968): 123–32.

Perrakis, Phyllis Sternberg (ed.). *Adventures of the Spirit: The Older Woman in the Works of Doris Lessing, Margaret Atwood, and Other Contemporary Women Writers*. Columbus: Ohio State University Press, 2007.

Rigney, Barbara Hill. *Madness and Sexual Politics in the Feminist Novel: Studies in Brontë, Woolf, Lessing and Atwood*. Madison: University of Wisconsin Press, 1978.

Sandler, Linda (ed.). *Margaret Atwood: A Symposium, The Malahat Review*, 41 January 1977.

Showalter, Elaine. 'Women and the Literary Curriculum', *College English* 32.8 (1971): 855–62.

Secondary sources

Biographies

Cooke, Nathalie. *Margaret Atwood: A Biography*. Toronto: ECW Press, 1998.

Sullivan, Rosemary. *The Red Shoes: Margaret Atwood Starting Out*. Toronto: HarperCollins, 1998.

Selected recommended criticism and reference works

Bouson, J. Brooks. *Brutal Choreographies: Oppositional Strategies and Narrative Design in the Novels of Margaret Atwood*. Amherst: University of Massachusetts Press, 1993.

Cooke, Nathalie. *Margaret Atwood: A Critical Companion*. Greenwood, 2004.

Davey, Frank. *Margaret Atwood: A Feminist Poetics*. Vancouver: Talonbooks, 1984.

Davidson, Arnold E. and Cathy N. Davidson. *The Art of Margaret Atwood*. New York: MLA, 1981.

Fleenor, Juliann E. (ed.). *The Female Gothic*. Montreal: Eden Press, 1983.

Grace, Sherrill and Lorraine Weir. *Margaret Atwood: Language, Text and System*. Vancouver: UBC, 1983.

Hengen, Shannon. *Margaret Atwood's Power: Mirrors, Reflections and Images in Select Fiction and Poetry*. Toronto: Second Story, 1993.

Hengen, Shannon, and Ashley Thomson. *Margaret Atwood: A Reference Guide*. Lanham, MD: Scarecrow Press, 2007.

Howells, Coral Ann (ed.). *The Cambridge Companion to Margaret Atwood*. Cambridge: Cambridge University Press, 2006.

Contemporary Canadian Women's Fiction: Refiguring Identities. Houndmills: Palgrave, 2003.

Margaret Atwood. 2nd edn. Houndmills: Palgrave, 2005.

Private and Fictional Words. London: Virago, 1987.

Howells, Coral Ann, and Lynette Hunter (eds.). *Narrative Strategies in Canadian Literature: Feminism and Post-Colonialism.* New York: Taylor & Francis, 1991.

Ingersoll, Earl G. *Waltzing Again: New and Selected Conversations with Margaret Atwood.* Princeton, NJ: Ontario Review Press, 2006.

Kroetsch, Robert, and Reingard M. Nischik (eds.). *Gaining Ground: European Critics on Canadian Literature.* Edmonton: NeWest Press, 1985.

Macpherson, Heidi Slettedahl. *Courting Failure: Women and the Law in Twentieth-Century Literature.* Akron: University of Akron Press, 2007.

Women's Movement: Escape as Transgression in North American Feminist Fiction. Amsterdam: Rodopi, 2000.

McCombs, Judith (ed.). *Critical Essays on Margaret Atwood.* Boston: Hall, 1988.

McWilliams, Ellen. *Margaret Atwood and the Female Bildungsroman.* Farnham: Ashgate, 2009.

Mendez-Egles, Beatrice. *Margaret Atwood: Reflection and Reality.* Edinburg, TX: Pan American University, 1987.

Mycak, Sonia. *In Search of the Split Subject: Psychoanalysis, Phenomenology, and the Novels of Margaret Atwood.* Toronto: ECW Press, 1996.

Nicholson, Colin (ed.). *Margaret Atwood: Writing and Subjectivity.* Houndmills: Palgrave, 1994.

Nischik, Reingard M. (ed.). *Margaret Atwood: Works and Impact.* Rochester, NY: Camden House, 2000.

Rao, Eleonora. *Strategies for Identity: The Fiction of Margaret Atwood.* New York: Peter Lang, 1993.

Rigney, Barbara Hill. *Margaret Atwood.* Houndmills: Macmillan, 1987.

Rosenberg, Jerome. *Margaret Atwood.* Boston: Twayne, 1984.

Stein, Karen. *Margaret Atwood Revisited.* New York: Twayne, 1999.

Tolan, Fiona. *Margaret Atwood: Feminism and Fiction.* Amsterdam: Rodopi, 2007.

Van Spanckeren, Kathryn, and Jan Garden Castro (eds.). *Margaret Atwood: Vision and Forms.* Carbondale: Southern Illinois University Press, 1988.

Wilson, Sharon Rose. *Margaret Atwood's Fairy-Tale Sexual Politics.* Jackson: University of Mississippi Press, 1993.

(ed.). *Margaret Atwood's Textual Assassinations.* Ohio State University Press, 2004.

Wilson, Sharon R., Thomas B. Friedman and Shannon Hengen. *Approaches to Teaching Atwood's The Handmaid's Tale and Other Works.* New York: Modern Language Association, 1996.

Wynne-Davies, Marion. *Margaret Atwood.* Tavistock: Northcote Publishing, 2009.

York, Lorraine. *Various Atwoods: Essays on the Later Poems, Short Fictions and Novels.* Toronto: Anansi, 1995.

Index

Cambridge Introductions to...